FUNDAMENTALS *of*
Mobile Marketing

This book is part of the Peter Lang Media and Communication list.
Every volume is peer reviewed and meets
the highest quality standards for content and production.

PETER LANG
New York • Washington, D.C./Baltimore • Bern
Frankfurt • Berlin • Brussels • Vienna • Oxford

SHINTARO OKAZAKI

FUNDAMENTALS *of* Mobile Marketing

THEORIES AND PRACTICES

PETER LANG
New York • Washington, D.C./Baltimore • Bern
Frankfurt • Berlin • Brussels • Vienna • Oxford

Library of Congress Cataloging-in-Publication Data
Okazaki, Shintaro.
Fundamentals of mobile marketing: theories and practices / Shintaro Okazaki.
p. cm.
Includes bibliographical references.
1. Internet marketing. 2. Mobile commerce.
3. Mobile communication systems. 4. Telemarketing. I. Title.
HF5415.1265.O348   658.8'72—dc23   2012016195
ISBN 978-1-4331-1562-2 (hardcover)
ISBN 978-1-4331-1561-5 (paperback)
ISBN 978-1-4539-0843-3 (e-book)

Bibliographic information published by **Die Deutsche Nationalbibliothek**.
Die Deutsche Nationalbibliothek lists this publication in the "Deutsche
Nationalbibliografie"; detailed bibliographic data is available
on the Internet at http://dnb.d-nb.de/.

The paper in this book meets the guidelines for permanence and durability
of the Committee on Production Guidelines for Book Longevity
of the Council of Library Resources.

© 2012 Peter Lang Publishing, Inc., New York
29 Broadway, 18th floor, New York, NY 10006
www.peterlang.com

Printed in the United States of America

To Amadeo

Contents

Preface

The convergence of the Internet and mobile telephony in the late 1990s produced a revolutionary telecommunication service: mobile Internet. Global mobile operators are now accelerating the technological transition from 2G to 3G and 4G. As a result, mobile marketing has quickly evolved into a strategic issue among firms seeking ubiquitous, interactive, and personalized marketing channels. Many brands and media companies are now engaged in sophisticated marketing promotions, proactively approaching mobile users and devices through a wide range of wireless technologies.

Mobile marketing began in the late 1990s with the sending of simple messages through SMS (Short Message Service). However, since the introduction and proliferation of the smartphone—in particular, the iPhone, the Android, and the BlackBerry—the strategy has changed. Through their mobile platforms, many mobile operators now offer a broad range of mobile applications and related transaction services, as well as a wide variety of informational and entertainment services. Still, many consider mobile marketing to be a young, immature form of online marketing. Considering its initial overhype during the early 2000s, a question arises as to what we can really learn from its resurgence. Has its time finally come?

We believe that electronic marketing through a mobile device is no longer a "new trend." The multifunctional touchscreen drastically increased sales in content downloads. As of this writing, Apple has surpassed the 10 billion application downloads by iPhone, iPod touch, and iPad users in only about 30 months (FierceDeveloper, 2011). Furthermore, sales revenues from smartphone applications, including iPhone, Android, and BlackBerry, are projected to exceed US$15 billion by 2013, up from $1.94 billion in 2009 (Market Watch, 2011b). In time, mobile marketing will grow in both quality and quantity, leaving ringtones and wallpaper downloads as prehistoric examples. Mobile marketing is helping to make ubiquitous computing a more realistic, everyday technology. This book is positioned at the heart of the issue: fundamental knowledge building of mobile marketing.

Mobile marketing defined

We need to begin by defining the term "mobile marketing." The Mobile Marketing Association, or MMA (2009), defines mobile marketing as "a set of practices that enables organizations to communicate and engage with their audience in an interactive and relevant manner through any mobile device or network." The critical point of this definition lies in two parts of its taxonomy:

1. The "set of practices" includes "activities, institutions, processes, industry players, standards, advertising and media, direct response, promotions, relationship management, CRM, customer services, loyalty, social marketing, and all the many faces and facets of marketing."
2. To "engage" means to "start relationships, acquire, generate activity, stimulate social interaction with organization and community members, [and] be present at time of consumers['] expressed need." Furthermore, engagement can be initiated by the consumer ("Pull") in form of a click or response or by the marketer ("Push"). (MMA, 2009)

The terms "mobile marketing" and "mobile commerce" sound the same, but they are slightly different. Loosely defined, mobile commerce (or m-commerce) is "the one or two-way exchange of value facilitated by a mobile consumer electronic device (e.g., a mobile handset) which is enabled by wireless technologies and communication networks" (MMA, 2010). The driver of this value exchange is mobile marketing. Without mobile marketing, neither selling nor buying would occur, since the existence of goods or services would not be communicated to consumers—hence no consumer response. Without marketing, we would not have any distribution channel that moves products and services from businesses to consumers. But the MMA definition implies that mobile marketing covers many more "faces and facets" of marketing, including public relations, events and experiences, CRM, and loyalty management.

Purpose of this book

In *Fundamentals of Mobile Marketing: Theories and Practices*, we have endeavored to combine theories and practices for college students as well as for experienced professionals. Our objective has been to identify, organize, and conceptualize relevant concepts in mobile marketing. Despite an increasing number of research publications in this field, many concepts have seldom been formally explicated. For that reason, this book focuses not only on tools and techniques but also on underlying theoretical explanations. Often, practices are the reasons behind theories, while theories guide practices. Pragmatic mobile marketing tools need to be understood in terms of "why," and knowing the reasons would help us to advance theories. On this basis, key aspects of mobile marketing that distinguish it from other forms of online marketing have been divided into eight chapters.

While mobile marketing books up to now have focused on general business issues, we have tried to balance theories and practices by providing historical background, widely recognized models, definitions, cutting-edge mobile technologies, and real-life examples. To back them up, we have conducted an extensive review of the academic literature and assembled a rich database of bibliographic references.

Organization

By blending academic theory and hands-on practice, the text focuses on the full range of mobile marketing tools. Throughout the book, current, up-to-date examples and issues are presented, along with examples of "Mobile Marketing in Action" for discussion.

Chapter 1, "Advances in Mobile Information Technology," provides basic information about Internet connectivity through mobile devices. Some background on 1G to 4G transition is provided, while technical terms relevant to mobile marketing are explained.

Chapter 2, "Technology Adoption and Diffusion Theories," highlights widely recognized theories and models associated with new technology adoption. We believe this information is necessary for a better understanding of mobile marketing, as its adoption and diffusion are key to this growing industry.

In Chapter 3, "Mobile Marketing Framework," we examine whether the scope of cloud computing can be extended to our contextualization of mobile marketing. A framework based on the interrelation among cloud-based marketing, 4Ps, and the consumer decision-making process is presented and explained as it pertains to an effective mobile marketing plan.

Chapter 4, "Ubiquity: Conceptualizing Time and Space," summarizes the most pronounced benefit of this communication device. Ubiquity is examined from the perspectives of different disciplines, including time-geography, psychology, and marketing. We also propose a further breakdown of its construct dimension.

In Chapter 5, "2D Codes and Near Field Communication," challenges to multichannel marketing tools are explicated. Key technologies in coding and wireless data exchange are introduced with illustrative examples.

Chapter 6, "Mobile Advertising and Promotion," provides an overview of the major tools and trends in advertising and promotion. Here we present a classification scheme framed by push/pull strategies and the level of consumer response.

Chapter 7, "Location-based Services," treats one of the most fascinating tools in mobile marketing. Issues related to location-based services are examined in terms of the tourism and health industries. The increasingly important topic of consumer privacy is also discussed.

Chapter 8, "Mobile Payment and Security," covers basic mobile payment tools and raises issues concerning virus and malware protection. To mobile marketers and advertisers, a lack of payment capability is a serious impediment, since it directly affects sales closure.

Specific advantages of this book

This is the first book in its field to provide comprehensive coverage of mobile marketing from both theoretical and managerial perspectives. The mobile device is presented not only as a communication medium but also as a transaction tool. Furthermore, mobile marketing is considered an essential integrated marketing force in emerging cloud-based holistic marketing.

Each chapter addresses three primary questions: (1) What is the primary theoretical foundation for the topic? (2) What is the current state of our research? and (3) What are the cutting-edge practices? In this way, we try to explicate key terms and their definitions. Our objective is to provide sufficient conceptualization of mobile marketing to enable better understanding of its diffusion and adoption behavior. In addition, because most of the existing books on mobile marketing (or mobile commerce) suffer from trying to take either too technical or too managerial a focus, we attempt to achieve an integration of both perspectives to provide a balanced view. For this reason, we hope that this book will be a useful reference tool for both academics and professionals engaged in this area of research. The book concludes with a comprehensive glossary of important terms that provides readers with concise definitions of key concepts.

Expected audience

This book is written for students, scholars, and practitioners interested in or engaged in mobile marketing. It can be used as a textbook for undergraduate or graduate courses in online marketing or online media management. (An introductory course in marketing is recommended as a pre-requisite.) A second audience is the large group of people taking non-university courses on specialized topics. Finally, this book is especially useful to managers requiring a theoretical view of the phenomenon of mobile marketing in order to keep abreast of the most recent developments in the field.

Acknowledgments

This book would never have materialized without the guidance, assistance, and encouragement of many of my mentors, colleagues, students, and practitioners with and from whom I have worked and learned over the years. I am truly indebted to the editor, Mary Savigar. Mary's professionalism, unflagging patience, and consistent support for the project made this book possible. I thank my production editor, Bernadette Shade, for her efficiency and precision. A very special word of appreciation goes to the Yoshida Hideo Memorial Foundation and the KDDI Foundation for their continuous support of my research that led to my fundamental knowledge of what mobile marketing really means. I also thank leading practitioners of D2 Communications, Tokyo, Japan, who provided me with plentiful opportunities to discuss the way in which mobile marketing is—and should be—conducted in the real world. Special thanks go to Barbara Mueller of San Diego State University for providing many useful suggestions for improvement. I would also like to extend my thanks to the Spanish Ministry of Science and Innovation (National Plan for Research, Development and Innovation EC02011–30105) for financial support in preparing the manuscript. A special word of appreciation goes to the many professionals who granted permission to reproduce their copyrighted materials.

Finally, I am deeply grateful to the students, professors, and professionals who will be using this book. I sincerely hope that it will add to their knowledge and expertise in the field of mobile marketing.

Shintaro Okazaki
Universidad Autónoma de Madrid
Madrid, Spain
March 2012

Advances in Mobile Information Technology

A new era in mobile marketing is quickly approaching. The explosion of mobile commerce has been fueled by rapid advances in mobile telephony and a steady transition toward 3G or even 4G mobile network technologies, producing many technical vocabularies. Thus, it may be helpful to learn key specialized terminology that is widely used in this field. To that end, this first chapter aims at establishing our basic knowledge of mobile information technology. The chapter starts with a clear definition of mobile marketing and then describes technological advances in mobile telecommunication systems from historical perspectives. Later, the author explains the past and present of the mobile Internet, followed by a current power map of major mobile operation systems.

Mobile telecommunication technologies

During the past decade we have witnessed unprecedented proliferation in mobile marketing practices. Besides "traditional" SMS (Short Message Service) and MMS (Multimedia Message Service) messaging functions, more personalized, context-aware, and value-added applications are available for mobile marketers and advertisers. Picture this: A hungry traveler drives through a city she has never visited before. Stopping at a gas station, she manages a GPS-based travel application in her mobile device that indicates several dining choices on an interactive map. A final click indicates the shortest driving route on a Google map and enables her to dial a phone number to make a reservation. Such a story is no longer a part of our future landscape. When compared with the "old days"—when most mobile marketing centered on text messaging and music or screensaver downloading—there is a new breed of mobile marketing through smartphones that ranges from banking to social networking.

Smartphones offer more advanced computing ability and Internet connectivity than a contemporary basic-feature phone, which is a low-end mobile phone that has less computing ability. In addition to their built-in functions (such as digital voice, text messaging, e-mail, Web browsing, camera, video, MP3 player, television, and organizer), smartphones have become mobile application delivery platforms, turning the once single-minded cell phone into a mobile computer. For example, a market research firm, In-Stat, projects as many as 48 billion mobile application downloads by 2015, due to Apple's App Store and Android Market, which offer more than 425,000 and 200,000 applications respectively (Computerworld, 2011). According to Apple, more than 15 billion App Store applications, were downloaded by 200 million iPhone, iPad, and iPod touch users worldwide over the past 3 years (Apple, 2011b). Google claims 4.5 billion app downloads from its Android Market to date (Android Community, 2011).

Thanks to smartphones, more than 33.3 million U.S. consumers already engage in shopping-related activities on their mobile phones, while 2.3 million of those consumers have made a purchase on their devices (Internet Retailer, 2011a). According to Forrester Research, 24% of U.S. adult online iPhone users and 21% of Android users have used a shopping application in the past 3 months (Internet Retailer, 2011b).

Looking back: Birth of SMS

It is highly tempting to say that "everything goes mobile." But without specific definitions and correct knowledge, we may end up with general confusion as to what kind of services are really available in mobile and what we expect from them. The objective of this chapter is therefore to provide a first step toward our understanding of mobile marketing by painting a general picture of advances in mobile information technology.

To date, there have been numerous phone devices and Personal Digital Assistants (PDAs) that have attempted to introduce "ubiquitous" Internet services. However, the most widely used data application on mobile phones remains SMS or text messaging. The total number of SMSs sent globally more than tripled between 2007 and 2010, from an estimated 1 trillion to a staggering 6.1 trillion. In other words, close to 200,000 text messages were sent every second. Assuming an average cost of US$0.07 per SMS, in 2010 SMS traffic generated an estimated US$14,000 every second. In 2009, SMS revenue accounted for 12% of China's largest mobile operator's total revenue (ITU, 2010).

Fig. 1.1. 15th Anniversary of SMS
This picture was taken at the party to celebrate the 15th SMS anniversary event in London in 2007. On December 3, 1992, Neil Papworth (pictured left) sent the world's first-ever commercial text message, "Merry Christmas," to Vodafone Director Richard Jarvis (right). Source: 160 Characters (2007).

SMS is a standard for telephony messaging systems that allow sending short messages—normally with text-only content—between mobile devices (MMA, 2009). Typing a touch-screen, keypad, or keyboard enters the text, and it may consist of words, numbers, or alphanumeric combinations. SMS was created as part of the Global System for Mobile Communication (GSM) Phase 1 standard. It uses the network-signaling channel for data transmitting and receiving. Therefore, SMS is an efficient communication medium that does not consume voice-communication channels and resources.

The first SMS message was sent from a computer to a mobile phone in 1992 in the U.K., while the first person-to-person SMS from phone to phone was sent in Finland in 1993. On December 3, 1992, a young engineer at Sema Group (now Airwide Solutions), Neil Papworth, sent the world's first-ever SMS message from his personal computer to Vodafone Director Richard Jarvis at a staff Christmas party. The first commercial deployment of an SMS Center was by Aldiscon (now Acision) with Telia (now TeliaSonera) in Sweden in 1993.

All initial installations of SMS gateways were to send network notifications to mobile phones, normally to inform of voice messages. The first commercially sold SMS service was offered to consumers as a person-to-person text messaging service by Radiolinja (now part of Elisa) in Finland in 1993. Other non-SMS data services were also launched, including ringtones, wallpapers, logos, pictures, gaming, gambling, adult entertainment, and advertising. The first commercial-grade mobile phone with ringtones was the Japanese NTT DoCoMo Digital Mova N103 HYPER by NEC, released in May 1996. Radiolinja introduced the first downloadable ringtone service in Finland in 1998. In 1999, Japanese mobile operator NTT DoCoMo launched its mobile Internet service, i-mode, with Fujitsu's Digital Mova F501i HYPER. In 2000, the world's first SMS news service began in Finland. Mobile payments were first trialed in Finland in 1998 when two Coca-Cola vending machines in Espoo were enabled to work with SMS payments.

The technology has evolved considerably since the days when there were many economic, social, and cultural barriers that impeded consumers' adoption of mobile marketing. In 2011, consumers are more likely to use a GPS application to update live traffic flow and incident reports or to redeem digital coupons at fast-food restaurants. Comparing now with a decade ago, there has been a drastic change in terms of user perception of mobile devices. When was the turning point? History may tell. But in the author's view, it was not until June 27, 2007, when Apple launched the first iPhone classic, that all awaited scenarios became a reality. This smartphone with multi-touch-screen capability completely changed our way of thinking about how mobile devices should and could be. Now, its intensifying battle with Google's Android smartphones provides important benefits to users, as they constantly improve the usability of the device. At the same time, such evolution of mobile computing technology makes the divide between mobile phones and computers less and less clear. For example, according to a recent survey, as many as 43% of the iPhone users consider the device "a computer that we can carry and bring to anywhere."

Before moving forward with our discussion on mobile information technology, it seems necessary to establish a historical and technical background on advances in the mobile communication industry. In the following sections, the author attempts to provide a panoramic view of generational changes, underpinning the revolutionary changes in mobile devices and infrastructure development.

TABLE 1.1. Evolution of Mobile Information Technology

Technology	Started	Description	Services	Standards	Data bandwidth	Core network
1G	1984	This generation of phones and networks is represented by the brick-sized analog phones introduced in the 1980s. Subsequent numbers refer to newer and upcoming technology.	Analog voice	NMT, AMPS, Hicap CDPD, TACS, and ETACS	1.9 kbps	P S T N [1]
2G	1991	2G phones use digital networks. Going all-digital allowed for the introduction of digital data services, such as SMS and e-mail. 2G networks and their digital nature also made it more difficult to eavesdrop on mobile phone calls.	Digital voice	GSM, CDMA, TDMA, iDEN, and PDC	14.4 kbps	PSTN
2.5G	1999	2.5G is a transition from 2G to 3G. In 2.5G, the most popular services such as SMS, GPRS, EDGE, High Speed Circuit switched data, and more had been introduced.	Higher capacity packetized data	GPRS, EDGE, etc.	384 kbps	PSTN, packet network
3G	2002	3G networks are an in-between standard. 3G is seen more as pre-4G instead of a standard of its own. The advantage 3G networks have over 2G networks is speed. 3G networks are built to handle the needs of today's wireless users. This standard of wireless networks increases the speed of Internet browsing, picture and video messaging, and handheld GPS use.	Higher capacity, broadband data up to 2 Mbps	CDMA, EV-DO, UMTS, and EDGE	2 Mbps	Packet network
4G	2011	4G (AKA Beyond 3G) is like the other generations in that its advantage lies in promised increased speeds in data transmission. There is currently no formal definition for 4G, but there are objectives. One of these objectives is for 4G to become a fully IP-based system, much like modern computer networks. The supposed speeds for 4G will be between 100 Mbit/s and 1 Gbit/s.	Completely IP based, speed up to hundreds of MBs	WIMAX2 and LTE Advanced	1 Gbit	Internet

1. Public Switched Telephone Network or PSTN is the network of the world's public circuit-switched telephone networks. It consists of telephone lines, fiber optic cables, microwave transmission links, cellular networks, communications satellites, and undersea telephone cables, all inter-connected by switching centers, thus allowing any telephone in the world to communicate with any other.

Source: Own elaboration based on 4G Americas (2011)

Progress from 1G to 2G

There are over 1.3 billion mobile phone users around the world, among which 40% access the Internet on a daily basis. This integration of cell phone and Internet, or mobile Internet, has quickly gained more and more users, especially since the penetration of 3G services. By the end of 2010, there were an estimated 5.3 billion mobile cellular subscriptions worldwide, including 940 million subscriptions to 3G services (ITU, 2010). This is in contrast to the previous eras of 1G and 2G when operators managed systems and technologies whose applications were limited to local markets. Here, 1G refers to the first-generation wireless services, most of which were *analog* technology standards (such as AMPS) that originated in 1981. By contrast, 2G, also known as Personal Communication Service (PCS), refers to the second-generation wireless services, which use *digital* mobile phone technologies that emerged during the 1990s, including Code Division Multiple Access (CDMA), Time Division Multiple Access (TDMA), and GSM, among others (MMA, 2009). The major advantage of 2G, compared with 1G, is to enable users to deliver both voice and data transmission, including such other auxiliary services as fax and SMS. The move from 1G to 2G transmission occurred in 1991 when GSM-based cellular telecom networks were commercially launched in Finland by Radiolinja in 1991. Nokia 1011, introduced on November 10, 1992, was the first GSM phone to go into mass production. It was adopted by U.K. mobile giants Vodafone and Cellnet (now 02).

Despite the improved functionality, 2G suffers from several major limitations in terms of mobile Internet support. First, it relies primarily on the circuit-switched transmission system, which requires slow setup time for each reconnection. Also, the circuit-switched system results in expensive usage charges, because users must maintain a communication channel for the entire duration of a data transmission. For example, in 2G systems, users must pay not only for the time to download e-mails or reserve a movie ticket but also for the time to compose messages or the time to browse and search the Web for a movie theater. That is, in 2G, users are required to reserve a specific physical path, regardless of whether it is actually being used. Because others cannot use this path, the operator needs to charge the entire connection time. In addition, low data rates, lack of integration with Internet protocols, and patchy security are other weaknesses of 2G systems (Sadeh, 2002).

These shortcomings worsened already-problematic usability issues of mobile Internet. In general, industry surveys of mobile Internet users echoed that major frustrations came from the many limitations of mobile devices, such as limited screen size, inconvenient input functionality due to extremely tiny keyboards, limited memory, and insufficient processing power. These features are in sharp contrast to the increasing usability of PC or wired Internet, where well-targeted content in colorfully presented Web sites generates a steady stream of e-commerce users.

3G proliferation

Overcoming these limitations of 2G standards, 2.5G mobile communication systems emerged. The umbrella term "2.5G" was used during the transition from 2G to 3G, when General Packet Radio Services (GPRS) technology was introduced as intermediate packet-switched systems. This was the first step toward *always-on* capacity. Instead of requiring a fixed allocation scheme, GPRS enables the number of time slots allocated to a channel to vary over time, while flexibly adjusting to actual traffic. This capacity allows much more efficient bandwidth utilization. Furthermore, the deployment of GPRS does not require any modification of any base station hardware. Compared with 2G, 2.5G offers the following advantages:

- Always-on data access functionality
- More efficient capacity consumption
- More flexible billing options
- Higher data rates

In the packet-switched transmission system, users can maintain an open connection and are only charged when they actually consume the capacity: hence, more flexible billing options. The term "packet" means "a small unit of data." Packets are routed through a network based on the destination address contained within each packet. Breaking down data transmission into packets allows users to share the data path with others in a network. Users are billed based on the number of packets; thus it is much more economical.

This packet-switched transmission system leads to "always-on" data access functionality. It is so called because users feel connected to the network without any interruption. "Always-on" communication offers two important benefits to mobile operators. First, it reduces costs. Second, it opens a new business opportunity to deliver real-time voice and data services in response to constantly changing customer needs.

3G, or the third generation wireless services, appeared in the late 1990s. On October 1, 2001, NTT DoCoMo in Japan introduced the Freedom of Mobile Multimedia Access (FOMA) service, which was the first commercial launch of 3G, although it was initially somewhat limited in scope; broader availability was delayed by apparent concerns over reliability. The second network to go commercially live was by SK Telecom in South Korea on the 1xEV-DO technology in January 2002. A 3G system must allow simultaneous use of speech and data services and provide peak data rates of at least 200 kbit/s, according to the IMT-2000 specification. Higher data speed supports a wide range of Internet and multimedia applications and services, including full motion video. The five principal concepts of 3G are as follows:

- Advanced commonality of system design on a global basis
- Service commonality within the IMT-2000 network and with the fixed network
- High-quality service with broad bandwidth and high speed (upwards of 2 Mbps)
- Small mobile terminals
- Global roaming capability throughout Europe, Japan, and North America

3G was first called FPLMTS (Future Public Land Mobile Telecommunication System) and then was renamed IMT-2000. IMT stands for International Mobile Telecommunication; 2000 refers to the year 2000, when the service was expected to start, as well as the number of the MHz frequency. However, the only IMT-2000 system that was fully operational in the first quarter of 2002 was NTT DoCoMo's 3G service, which went online in October 2001.

Depending on the type of 2G telecommunication system, different migration scenarios were painted by the operators. International Telecommunication Union (ITU) planned to implement a frequency band of 2000MHz globally. The International Mobile Telephone IMT-2000 supports technical analysis for high-speed telephone solutions. The world of wireless communication development arrives at GSM, IS-136, PDC, or CDMA.[1] The 3G evolution for CDMA systems brings CDMA2000. The 3G evolution for GSM, IS-136, and PDC systems leads to Wideband CDMA (W-CDMA), also known as Universal Mobile Telecommunication Service (UMTS). W-CDMA is based on the network fundamentals of GSM with the same improvement also implemented in GSM and IS-136 through EDGE.

UMTS is characterized by development in terms of various services and bandwidths. The evolution of these networks is based on the GSM/GPRS networks. UMTS networks support all types of applications, such as data, voice, and video. While IP is the driving technology, UMTS introduced a new radio access technology based on a radio access network without any major change to the core network.

GSM operators experience a relatively simple transition to a GSM-enhanced device with W-CDMA, which stands for Wideband Code-Division Multiple-Access, also referred to as UMTS Terrestrial Radio Access Network (UTRAN). W-CDMA/UMTS was developed by the third-generation partnership project (3GPP).

W-CDMA/UMTS was developed in the late 1990s by NTT DoCoMo as the air interface for its 3G network FOMA. Later the International Telecommunication Union (ITU) accepted W-CDMA/UMTS as an alternative to CDMA2000, EDGE, and the short-range DECT system, which belong to the IMT-2000 family of 3G standards. Compared with GPRS, W-CDMA/UMTS provides several benefits.

From 3G to 4G

4G, or the fourth generation of cellular wireless standards, is a successor to the 3G and 2G families of standards. 4G refers to all-IP packet-switched networks (i.e., end-to-end IP), mobile ultra-broadband (gigabit-speed) access, and multi-carrier transmission. Pre-4G technologies such as mobile WiMAX and first-release 3G Long Term Evolution (LTE) have been on the market since 2006 and 2009, respectively.

A 4G system is expected to provide a comprehensive and secure all-IP-based solution where facilities such as IP telephony, ultra-broadband Internet access, gaming services, and streamed multimedia may be provided to users. The full implementation of 4G is expected to enable pervasive computing, wherein simultaneous connections to multiple high-speed networks provide seamless handoffs throughout a given geographical area. Network operators may employ technologies such as cognitive radio and wireless mesh networks to ensure connectivity and efficiently distribute both network traffic and spectrum. The enhanced speeds of the 4G system will create new markets and opportunities for both traditional and startup telecommunications companies. 4G-enabled mobile phones equipped with higher-quality digital cameras (and even HD capabilities) will enable *vlogging*, or video blogging, Web television, and new models for collaborative citizen journalism. NTT DoCoMo is testing 4G communications at 100 Mbps for mobile users and up to 1 Gbps while stationary. NTT DoCoMo released its first commercial network in 2010.

Evolution of mobile Internet services

WAP

Wireless Application Protocol, or WAP, is not a protocol but rather a suite of protocols that bridge the gap between the variety of mobile bearer services and basic Internet protocols (such as TCP/IP and HTTP, the HyperText Transfer Protocol) commonly used to access Web pages over the fixed Internet. Earlier WAP (1.0, 1.1, and 1.2) required the introduction of a WAP gateway, which serves as an interface between the WAP protocol stack. WAP content is encoded into a compact binary format. When a user tries to enter a particular URL address in his or her mobile device, the WAP gateway decodes it into regular HTTP text and forwards it to the URL's server over the fixed Internet. The server then returns the script document to the gateway, which encrypts it and forwards it to the mobile device. However, because any communication must go through the WAP gateway, earlier WAP users experienced a high level of frustration because of slow connections, poorly managed sites, outdated content, and small screens. However, after the introduction of WAP2.0 in 2002, many of these problems were resolved, because it supports an alternative protocol stack that enables users to do away with the WAP gateway. However, the gateway is still necessary to support additional functionality such as billing, location-based services, or privacy features.

i-mode

NTT DoCoMo (Do Communications by Mobile) was founded in 1992 by the Japanese telecommunication giant NTT. At the time of its launch, the number of mobile subscribers was only 80,000, less than 1% of the total Japanese population. However, the penetration of mobile devices accelerated rapidly, reaching 44.6 million in 2003. The secret of NTT DoCoMo's drastic rise was in a mobile Internet service called "i-mode," short for "information mode," which was launched in February 1999. The i-mode is a "semi-walled garden" controlled by its packet network and server system. When users select i-mode, they are presented with an i-menu and links to personal information management applications, offering users a *one-stop shop* solution.

The i-mode accommodated diverse *killer apps*, such as built-in GPS, music downloads, videos, e-coupons for discounts, bill payment, and even karaoke. Strategically, this portal imposes no additional infrastructure costs, because the content creation can be arranged with a number of third-party content providers and aggregators. As a result, within 18 months of its launch, i-mode attracted more than 10 million subscribers. By 2001, the number of subscribers increased threefold to over 30 million. In 2004, NTT DoCoMo's group net profits more than tripled to 650 billion yen, and its competitors, Vodafone and au (KDDI's mobile operator), implemented similar mobile Internet services, albeit using different underlying technologies. E-mail is considered the most popular *killer app*, and 71% of i-mode users receive an e-mail newsletter.

However, what made i-mode so unique was its method of connecting to the Internet, in that it offers continuous Internet access based on packet-switching technology. Unlike WAP dialing into a modem, i-mode is "always on," and users pay "by the piece" for data rather than for air time. NTT DoCoMo charged a nominal monthly fee, approximately 300 yen (under US$3) a month, plus a fee for each data packet downloaded and uploaded to the handsets. Another unusual feature of i-mode is the way it develops i-mode content. Instead of purchasing the services, NTT DoCoMo allowed content providers to provide fee-based content and services with collection through NTT DoCoMo's subscription billing system, which offers multiple incentives for active content creation. In i-mode, while many different contents are structured into official (approved) and unofficial (non-approved) providers, only official providers can charge for content.

The i-mode was a precursor of a strategic business model in mobile commerce that places more emphasis on content, the value chain of content aggregation, its management, and access. However, one of the reasons why i-mode was so rapidly and widely accepted in Japan could be attributed, at least partially, to two main factors. First, in Japan, Internet connection in PCs was very expensive; therefore, there was a potential market for people eager to use online services with reduced fees. Second, in Japan, unlike in the United States, average workers use public transportation such as buses, trains, or subways extensively. The average commute time is 1.5 hours, oftentimes with changes in the mode of transportation. Voice calls are normally forbidden in these venues; thus there was a potential need for something to pass the time, which fitted i-mode-to-download contents, or the sending of e-mails.

By January 2004, "i-mode" subscribers numbered 44.7 million, while total users outside Japan exceeded 3 million (NTT DoCoMo, 2004). Its European user base had expanded through partnerships with key mobile operators, including E-Plus in Germany, KPN Mobile in the Netherlands, BASE in Belgium, Bouygues Telecom in France, Telefónica Móviles in Spain, WIND Telecomunicazioni in Italy, and COSMOTE in Greece. In the United States, DoCoMo was also engaged in the development of mobile multimedia business with AT&T Wireless (NTT DoCoMo, 2004). However, the expansion of the i-mode business model hardly came to fruition. One of the primary reasons for this was that 3G mobile service was still too expensive for continuous use in many countries. In addition, people did not see any special need to use mobile devices for Internet connection. Mobile Internet services are the most popular pastime among Japanese consumers when they are riding on public transportation. In contrast, European and American consumers primarily use cars, leaving little opportunity to play with mobile Internet (Baldi & Thaung, 2002). In Japan, the popularity of i-mode has also gradually declined since 2004, as au started attracting many users who sought more sophisticated design and usability.

iPhone revolution

The development and penetration of 3G were not necessarily parallel to the improvement of mobile handsets. In particular, a lack of interface usability—in information architecture, user-friendly navigation, graphics, keyboard functionality, and screen size—has been an important obstacle in mobile phones in general, and in mobile Internet services in particular. The majority of handsets developed in Japan were designed to appeal solely to domestic consumers, without any international expansion. This became known as the Galapagos effect, meaning that the Japanese super-powerful mobile ecosystem with futuristic technologies, business models, and experiences was carefully incubated in isolation and was so unique that it would evolve apart from outside influences (Mobile Media Monitor, 2011).

Apple CEO Steve Jobs broke new ground in 2007 when he introduced the *iPhone* during his keynote address at the Macworld Conference and Expo. During the 2-year development period for the iPhone, Jobs embarked on a campaign to sign a wireless company as the exclusive carrier for the iPhone. Eventually, he was able to convince AT&T to abandon almost all control over the development of the iPhone to the point where only three executives at AT&T had seen the iPhone before it was announced (Sharma, Wingfield, & Yuan, 2007). This situation gave Apple the liberty to develop its product on its own terms and to keep its features under tight wraps.

One industry expert describes the moment when Steve Jobs presented the iPhone for the first time:

> Then, Jobs touched the screen. Suddenly, the featureless rectangle screen became an interactive surface. Jobs placed a fingertip on an on-screen arrow and slid it from left to right. When his finger moved, the arrow moved with it, unlocking the phone. To some people, this interaction between a human finger and an on-screen image—and its effect on the iPhone's behavior—was more amazing than all of its other features combined. (Wilson, 2007)

In some ways the iPhone is more like a palmtop computer than a cellular phone. But most of all, it is a long-awaited smartphone that enables users to make and receive calls, watch movies, take pictures and video, listen to music, browse the Web, and send and receive e-mail and text messages with just a fingertip. It is the usability issue. Apple revolutionized the whole concept of mobile telecommunication by developing multi-touch technology for the iPhone screen. It may not be an exaggeration that it was not until Apple introduced this easy, intuitive, and practical keyboard-free system to the market that our dreams of personalized, location-sensitive, and content-aware applications really came into being. During the first weekend after its launch, approximately 3 billion programs were downloaded. This explosive figure alone not only illustrates the enthusiastic iPhone 3G acceptance but also reflects the long-lasting frustration of more "traditional" mobile device users.

In 2008, the second-generation iPhone 3G was released, which can operate on 3G networks and has a GPS receiver. This version also lets users view map and satellite data from Google Maps, including overlays of nearby businesses. In 2009, Apple launched the iPhone 3GS, which had greater storage capacity and a better camera capable of taking still shots and video at 30 frames per second. Another new feature is a compass, which comes in handy when you need to find your way through unfamiliar territory. Also in 2009 came iPhone OS 3.0, which offered many improvements, such as the ability to cut and paste.

In a way, Apple's iPhone followed the i-mode "semi-walled garden" business model. The service strategy is planned around a portal called "iTunes" where users are required to be registered in order to download free or paid applications at the App Store. The applications are accessible directly through PC and passed on to an iPhone through a process called "synchronization" with a USB cable. Mobile Internet connection can be set up either directly in the phone or indirectly (via iTune synchronization from PC), enabling users to access e-mails, Web sites, GPS, and numerous other applications. The iTunes software is designed to perform three basic functions:

- Browse + Buy: Buy music and more at the App Store.
- Collect + Play: Import CDs, organize and play content.
- Sync + Go: Sync content to the iPhone.

Several universities, including Stanford University, the University of Wisconsin-Madison, and the University of California-Berkeley, are now using a customized iTunes Store known as iTunes U to deliver educational content to students and faculty. Businesses are evaluating the use of iTunes to deliver targeted and general corporate communications and training to desktops and iPods to deliver information to executives (Carden, 2007).

On June 23, 2010, Apple launched iPhone 4 (fourth generation), the successor to the iPhone 3GS. It is particularly marketed for video calling; for consumption of media such as books and periodicals, movies, music, and games; and for general Web and e-mail access. In October 2011, Apple unveiled iPhone 4S which retains the exterior design of iPhone 4 but supports both GSM and CDMA networks connectivity iOS 5 with a range of improved hardware specifications and software updates.

TABLE 1.2. Comparison between iPad and Kindle

Criteria	iPad	Kindle W
OS	iPhone OS	Kindle OS
Size	Height: 242.8 mm Width: 187.7 mm Depth: 13.4 mm	Height: 264.16 mm Width: 182.88 mm Depth: 9.65 mm
Weight	680.3 g	289.1 g
Processing speed and capacity	1Ghz CPU, 16GB, 32GB, 64GB, flash drive	3.3GB or User Available Memory
Cellular and wireless	GSM/GPRS/EDGE, Wi-Fi, Bluetooth 2.1 + EDR	AT&T 3G
Power and battery	Lithium-ion battery, 10 hours of web on Wi-Fi, video and music	1 Week reading time with Wi-Fi on, 2–3 weeks with Wi-Fi off
Display	9.7 inch (diagonal) with 1024 x 768 resolution	9.7 inch with E-Ink Technology with 1200 x 824 resolution
Multi-touch capacity	Yes	No
Keyboard	Onscreen virtual keyboard	Physical QWERTY keyboard
Applications	200,000 + (iTunes App Store)	< 10
Books	iBooks + Kindle eBooks	Amazon Kindle Store (400,000+ books, magazines, and newspapers)

Sources: Based on Apple (2011c) and Amazon.com (2011)

Tablet and e-book

In April 2010, Apple launched a new tablet computer called *iPad*, which is a touch-panel-based PC with a 9.7-inch, high-resolution, multi-touch-capability screen. It operates only by finger touch, running the same operating system (OS) as the earlier iPhone and iPod 2G. The peculiarity of iPad lies in its positioning as a new telecommunication medium whose appearance, size, weight, and functionality meld laptop, smartphone, and gaming console. Apple had sold over 25 million iPads by June 2011 (About.com, 2011). The second generation or *iPad2* was released in March 2011.

With iPad, users can connect to the Internet via 3G or Wi-Fi for fast cellular network access. In terms of mobile Internet services, the App Store offers almost 200,000 iPhone applications for iPad. The most important application among them is iBook, which makes iPad the most powerful competitor for Amazon's Kindle, Barnes & Noble's NOOK, and Sony's Reader. The market for e-readers has been expanding at an astonishing pace. IDC estimates 10.8 million e-readers shipped worldwide in 2010, and that figure should grow to 14.7 million in 2011 (CNET, 2011), reaching an expected 67 million in 2016.

As of July 2010, Amazon announced that its sales of e-books more than tripled in the first half of 2010, as compared to one year before. The company said that in the past 3 months it had sold 143 Kindle books for every 100 hardcover books, while in July, sales of e-books accelerated to 180 sold for every 100 hardcover versions. Market analysts said the news was Amazon's attempt to tell investors that when it comes to the sale of e-books and e-readers, it is far ahead in the competition with iPad. According to Jefferies & Company's managing director Youssef H. Squali, Amazon's latest sales figures are "clearly an indication that the iPad is complementary to the Kindle, not a replacement" (Miller, 2011). In other words, many consumers do not see the iPad as comparable to the Kindle in terms of a reading device, but strong sales of iPad and Kindle reveal that people want to own both.

Android

Android is a software stack for mobile devices that includes an operating system, middleware, and key applications, and is based upon the Linux kernel and GNU software. It was initially developed by Android Inc., which was later purchased by Google, and lately broadened to the Open Handset Alliance. The Android software development kit provides the tools and libraries necessary to begin developing applications that run on Android-powered devices. According to Canalys, Android has increased phone shipments 886% since Q2 2009, and has the top market share of 33%, compared to the iPhone's 22%, among new smartphone purchasers. However, among current subscribers thinking of switching devices, the iPhone remains the most desired phone, finding loyalty with nearly 90% of current iPhone users and enticing healthy slices of Android users (21%) and BlackBerry owners (29%) to consider the move to Apple. Android's loyalty among switchers (71%) outperforms BlackBerry (42%), half of whose users could potentially chose an iPhone or an Android phone for their next device (Nielsenwire, 2010).

Industry analysts point out a number of differences between iPhone and Android. For example, there is a big difference in terms of the number of applications available for each platform: 230,000 in the App Store versus 70,000 in the

16 | *Fundamentals of Mobile Marketing*

TABLE 1.3. Comparison Between iPhone and Android (%)

Activities	iPhone	Android
Took photos	82.2	80.4
Used network services for photos/videos	65.6	63.1
Transferred photo to PC	59.4	52.8
Accessed social networking site or blog	56.0	51.1
Sent photo directly to another phone	47.1	55.0
Uploaded photo to Web	39.8	38.0
Captured video	25.3	47.8
Uploaded video to PC	22.6	31.5
Sent video directly to another phone	20.3	26.6
Sent video via e-mail	19.5	26.2
Uploaded video to Web	19.3	26.0

Source: PCWorld (2009)

Android platform. However, in the 10 most important application categories, iPhone and Android are almost even. iPhone's enormous App Store application lineup does not help it in certain situations where Apple has not been so open to its development community. In contrast, Android OS is freely available to anyone who builds hardware, allowing various carriers to sell Android phones with a variety of screen sizes and processor speeds. This provides game designers with an enormous advantage, especially because iPhone renews its model only once a year with a series of restrictions. For example, when Apple released iPhone OS version 4 on June 24, 2010, developers had to click on an "I agree" button to indicate acceptance of 50 pages of legalese before using a new software development kit. On the other hand, there is serious developer concern about the overwhelming number of free applications in Google's disorganized Android Market. According to the mobile applications tracking firm Distino, free downloads account for well over half the apps, including popular ones made by Google itself.

If Android owners are slightly more Web enabled, iPhone fans are slightly more social. Perceptive reviewers have, however, taken the iPhone to task for not being a very friendly social networking platform. It can be set up to get alerts from Facebook and Twitter, but users cannot really browse their feeds in a comfortable way without diving deep into the applications. As Table 1.3 shows, iPhone users come out on top when it comes to the most advanced social-oriented phone activities—everything from sharing photos to spending time on social networks and blogs. Only in video-specific social activity does the Android clan pull ahead again, with significantly higher percentages of users capturing video and sharing it over the Internet.

As an example of Android's Web capabilities, Motorola's Cliq is one of the most networking-focused smartphones produced to date. The Cliq does have a 5 megapixel camera and a full QWERTY keyboard, but the difference from other smartphones is its MOTOBLUR user interface. MOTOBLUR is a customized build of the Android operating system that uses an extensive concentration on inter-activity to the Internet for expansive networking capabilities. It brings updates, e-mails, messages, personal information, media, contacts, and more from all of one's online networking locations to a cleverly streamlined interactive output.

Current power map of mobile OS

While iPhone and Android are two major smartphones, there are other popular brands, such as Canadian RIM's (Research in Motion) BlackBerry, Finnish Nokia's S60/S40 series, and mobile phones running on Microsoft's Windows Mobile. The future map of mobile Internet services will be determined largely by the types of applications that can be used in mobile devices. By definition, smartphones should be tied into the operating system and hardware of the mobile device. Thus, it is the operating system that classifies smartphones. In addition to Apple's iPhone OS and Google's Android, there are Nokia's Symbian, RIM's BlackBerry OS, Microsoft's Windows Mobile, and Barm's Web OS. Nokia released Maemo, a new OS, in August 2009.

For each OS, there is an online application market wherein in-house or third-party vendors such as software firms and individual programmers sell mobile applications. The largest market is Apple's App Store, which has more than 200,000 applications registered. Nokia and RIM have created similar markets. For each market, the third-party vendors can develop applications using a software development kit provided by the sponsor firms that support each OS. When they sell these applications, firms receive 20–30% of the sales as a commission. However, the presence of Symbian and BlackBerry is getting smaller, as iPhone and Android have increased their shares in recent years (Nielsenwire, 2011).

TABLE 1.4. Applications and Markets for Smartphones

Company	OS	Start date and hardware	Market	Main characteristics	Description
Apple	iOS 5.X	October 2011; iPhone, iPad, and iPod	App Store	Closed source, multi-tasking, multi-screen interface, 4G LTE support, over-the-air updates	According to a preview in June 2011, a USB connection to iTunes is no longer necessary. Data synchronization happens automatically and wirelessly through iCloud service. A proprietary messaging app across all iOS devices and full Twitter integration.
Google	Android 3.X	May 2011; Any hardware manufacturer	Android Market	Open source, multi-tasking, multi-touch interface, over-the-air updates	Optimized tablet support and quick access to notifications, status, and soft navigation buttons available at the bottom of the screen. Action Bar allows access to contextual options, navigation, widgets, or other types of content at the top of the screen.
RIM	BlackBerry OS 7	August 2011; BlackBerry smartphones	BlackBerry App World	Closed source, multi-tasking, multi-touch model available	The browser has been "significantly enhanced" with new features like a JIT (just-in-time) JavaScript compiler and HTML5 Video support.
Microsoft	Windows Phone 7	October 2010; Windows Mobile-licensed mobile devices	Windows Marketplace for Mobile	Closed source, restricted multi-tasking, multi-touch interface, Internet Explorer	Windows Phone 7 is the successor to Microsoft's line of Windows Mobile phone operating systems. It is based on the Windows CE 6 kernel, like the Zune HD, while current versions of Windows Mobile are based on Windows CE5.
Palm	webOS 3.X	July 2011; Palm smartphones	Palm App Catalog	Closed source, multi-tasking, multi-touch interface, over-the-air updates	Initially developed by Palm, which was later acquired by Hewlett-Packard. However, on August 18, 2011, HP announced that it would discontinue production of all WebOS-related hardware devices.
Nokia	Symbian^3	February 2010; Nokia mobile devices	Ovi Store	Open source, visual multi-tasking, multi-touch interface, Mozilla browser	Nokia announced the cessation of sales of both its Symbian-based phones and feature phones in North America as it attempts to migrate to Windows Phone 7. Accenture will provide Symbian-based software development and support services through 2016.

Source: Based on data from each OS.

Summary

This chapter gives a panoramic overview of the advances of mobile telecommunication technologies. It starts with a clear definition of mobile marketing. We adopt a 2009 MMA definition of mobile marketing: "a set of practices that enables organizations to communicate and engage with their audience in an interactive and relevant manner through any mobile device or network." We then briefly describe the transitions from 1G to 4G, followed by a section explaining various phases of mobile Internet evolution, including the development of Wireless Application Protocol (WAP) and i-mode, iPhone, iPad, and Android, among others. In closing, a current map of mobile OS in which mobile applications run is discussed.

NOTE

1. The Personal Digital Cellular or Pacific Digital Cellular (PDC) system is a second-generation mobile phone technology introduced in 1991 in Japan. It uses Time Division Multiple Access (TDMA) technology, and it is very similar to the US "TDMA" or IS-136 system.

2

Technology Adoption
AND Diffusion Theories

The importance of theory in conducting research on the mobile Internet cannot be overstated. A theory is the language that allows us to move from observation to observation and make sense of similarities and differences. Researchers need such a language in order to interpret and understand the complex psychology and behavior of mobile marketing adopters. More formally, a theory can be defined as "a set of interrelated constructs (variables), definitions, and propositions that presents a systematic view of phenomena by specifying relations among variables, with the purpose of explaining natural phenomena" (Kerlinger, 1979, p. 64). In this light, our propositions, or hypotheses, should always exist within a theoretical framework and should specify the relationship among variables in terms of magnitude and/or direction.

Theories are not born overnight. Instead, they develop over time, after researchers thoroughly test a prediction. It is therefore our role to relate existing facts to a theory. For that reason, researchers are often interested in bridging independent, mediating, moderating, and dependent variables, trying to provide overarching explanations about their relationships.

In this regard, researchers have extended widely accepted existent behavioral models in attempts to explain the adoption of mobile marketing. The reason for this is in part to reconcile the many existent theories in PC or fixed Internet. In fact, many earlier explorations on m-commerce research focused on the question of how to apply existing e-commerce theories or models by introducing additional constructs that may substantiate the differences between wireless and wired Internet. Our true challenge arises when we try to go beyond this transition to find the real uniqueness of mobile Internet. In this chapter, we review some of the most representative theories and models related to new technology adoption. We hope that such theoretical knowledge will help readers to better understand why and how mobile marketing could be adopted and extended.

Descriptive theories

Diffusion of innovations

An innovation is defined as something new to the people to whom it is being introduced. Contemporary research on the diffusion of innovations stems from Gabriel Tarde, a 19th-century French sociologist and legal scholar. His book *The Laws of Imitation* introduced his theories and observations, which are regarded as the origins of such diffusion concepts as opinion leadership, the S-curve of diffusion, and the role of socio-economic status in interpersonal diffusion. In a descriptive definition, diffusion is the spread of social or cultural properties from one society or environment to another.

One of the most widely used theories is the diffusion of innovations by Rogers (1976). By 2003, more than 5,000 articles had been published on this theory. In September 2011, a search by Google Scholar with a keyword "diffusion of innovations" hit 32,000 citations. Rogers defines diffusion as the "process by which an innovation is communicated through certain channels over a period of time among the members of a social system." The social system could vary from virtually the entire society to a group of housewives in a particular district. An innovation is "an idea, practice, or product perceived to be new by the relevant individual or group." It is the perception of the potential market, not an objective measure of technological change, that determines whether a given product is innovative or not. The diffusion process typically involves both mass media and interpersonal communication channels. And, in today's world, information technologies such as the Internet and mobile phones, which combine aspects of both mass media and interpersonal channels, represent formidable tools of diffusion. Figure 2.1 summarizes the main components and their relationships in diffusion of innovations theory (Rice, 2009).

As a starting point, a social system encompasses social structures, economic cycles, regulatory policies, and industry trends, which are transmitted by interpersonal communication as well as media. An individual in a social system may become aware or informed of what kinds of innovations are available and to whom. The process of innovation development, which captures consumers' needs and problems—conscious and unconscious—by conducting market research, is often studied in marketing literature. Innovations stem from these needs and problems, and potential adopters are individuals, groups, communities, organizations, and governments who exhibit similar perceptions and behavioral patterns.

In these processes, potential adopters develop certain perceptions of the innovation characteristics. The most commonly cited are five general characteristics. A variety of diffusion studies have shown that these characteristics consistently influence adoption. Rogers (1976) defined them as follows:

- Relative Advantage: This attribute refers to the degree to which an innovation is perceived as being better than existing alternatives. That is, the better the innovation is perceived to meet the relevant need compared to its precursor, the more rapid the diffusion.
- Compatibility: This attribute means the degree to which an innovation is perceived as fitting the existing values, needs, and past experiences of an individual or group. That is, the more the purchase and use of the innovation is consistent with potential adopters' values or beliefs, the more rapid the diffusion will be.
- Complexity: This attribute can be defined as the degree to which an innovation is perceived as being difficult to use. That is, the more difficult it is to understand and use the innovation, the slower the diffusion will be.
- Trialability: This attribute can be defined as the degree to which an innovation may be experimented with before adoption. That is, the easier it is to have a low-cost or low-risk trial of the innovation, the more rapid its diffusion will be.
- Observability: This attribute refers to the degree to which the results of an innovation are observable to others. That is, the more easily consumers can observe the positive effects of adopting an innovation, the more rapid the diffusion will be.

These characteristics and social contexts of the potential adopters, along with the stages and outcomes of the initiation and implementation processes, determine one's adoption category, which in turn influences the timing, extent, and form of the adoption. According to Rogers (1976), consumers tend to create and share information with one another to reach a mutual understanding. The diffusion process is considered to revolve around four key elements: an innovation, communication channels to spread knowledge of the innovation, the length of time during which the diffusion takes place, and a social system of potential adopters. Opinion leaders exert influence on audience behavior via their personal contact, but additional intermediaries called change agents and gatekeepers are also included in the process of diffusion. The five adopter categories are: (1) innovators, (2) early adopters, (3) early majority, (4) late majority, and (5) laggards. Figure 2.2 shows the cumulative S-curve and adopter categories (Mathur, Chikkatur, & Sagar, 2007). The S-curve describes a general tendency of technology diffusion in the marketplace.

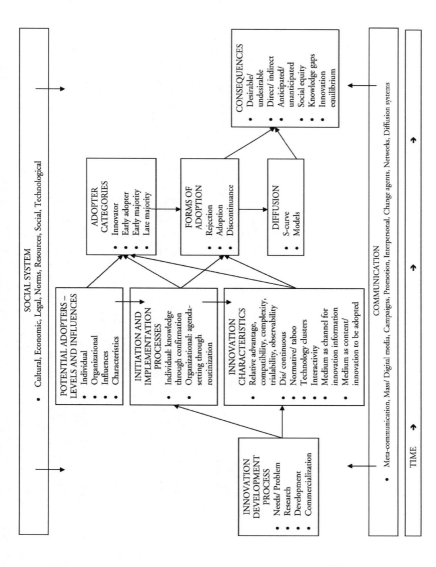

Fig. 2.1. Main Components of Diffusion of Innovations Theory. Source: Rice (2009, p. 490). Reproduced by permission.

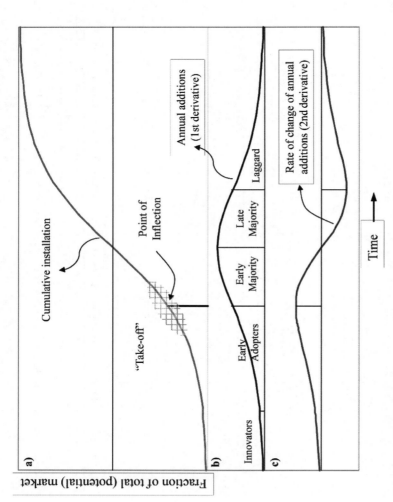

Fig. 2.2. The Cumulative S-curve and Adopter Categories.

Note: The curve denotes the cumulative number of technology adoptions as a function of time. (a) The "take-off" occurs generally at about 10–20% of the total adoption (as indicated by the cross-hatched area). (b) The various adopter categories are shown on a normal distribution curve that indicates the annual technology additions. (c) The maximum in the first derivative of the annual installation curve (i.e., the second derivative of the cumulative installation curve) indicates the first point of inflection in the annual installation curve, which in turn corresponds to the take-off region. Source: Mathur et al. (2007, p. 233). Reproduced by permission.

Uses and gratifications theory

The next descriptive theory is based on the well-established media uses and gratifications (U&G) paradigm. The U&G theory was originally developed by communications researchers to understand consumers' motivations to use different media. The U&G theory explains why individuals often seek out media in a goal-setting fashion to fulfill a core set of motivations, acknowledging that media users control their own decisions. It has been proven to be an axiomatic theory, because its principles are generally accepted, and it is readily applicable to a wide range of situations involving media communications.

U&G theory aims to explain the psychological needs that motivate people to engage in media use behaviors and to derive gratification from satisfying those intrinsic needs, under a particular socio-cultural environment. Lin (1999) explains the basic underlying assumptions of U&G theory as follows:

> . . . individuals differ along several psychological dimensions which, in turn, prompt them to make different choices about which media to patronize, and . . . even individuals exposed to the same media content will respond to it in different ways, depending on their characteristics.

Furthermore, U&G theory assumes that consumers are (1) goal-oriented in their behavior, (2) active media users, and (3) aware of their needs and select media to gratify those needs (Katz, Blumler, & Gurevitch, 1974). Figure 2.3 summarizes the fundamental components, structure, and functions of this theory (Lin, 1999).

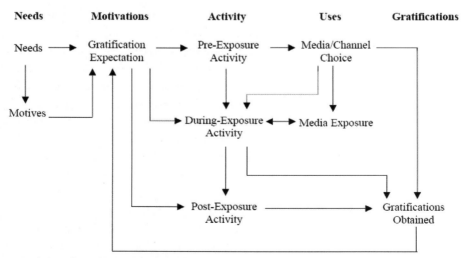

Fig. 2.3. Based on Uses and Gratifications Paradigm. Source: Lin (1999).

Media use needs can be understood as self-actualization needs, which develop independently from other people for need-fulfillment and can improve one's self-development. In general, five different self-actualization needs are thought to be relevant to U&G theory: (1) cognitive needs (the need to understand); (2) affective needs (the need to strengthen one's emotional experience); (3) integrative needs (the need to strengthen one's confidence, credibility, or stability); (4) contact needs (the need to strengthen relationships with family, friends, and the world); and (5) escape or tension-release needs.

Motives created by these needs vary among individuals, according to different socio-demographic backgrounds. Lin (1999) and Rubin (1983) argue that motives can cover some or all of the following dimensions:

- Entertainment: to seek fun, amusement, or excitement
- Surveillance: to keep up with what's going on in the world
- Information: to learn about things that are interesting and useful
- Diversion: to redirect one's attention to the "media reality"
- Escape: to forget about the problem at hand
- Social interaction: to have something to do with or say to others
- Parasocial interaction: to "talk back" to media personalities
- Identity: to find people or ideologies with which to identify
- Pass time: to relieve boredom and kill time
- Companionship: to reduce the feeling of loneliness

Needs and motives both influence the formation of motivations. Motivations describe the type of perceived incentives or rewards that can drive an individual to choose and engage in media use (Lin, 1999). Motivations are made up primarily of cognitive and affective dimensions. The cognitive dimension relates to the thoughts surrounding the gratifications that an individual expects or looks for when engaging in media use. In contrast, the affective dimension refers to an individual's emotional inclination toward the gratifications that he or she expects or seeks when first using a media channel. Cognitive and affective motivations drive an individual to initiate and execute media use activity. This process usually involves three phases: pre-, during-, and post-exposure activities.

Pre-exposure activity corresponds to preparation for media usage. For example, we often check several search engines, such as Yahoo! or Google, when "surfing" the Internet and deciding where to view the searched items.

During-exposure activity is that which occurs simultaneously with media use. It reflects the degree of user involvement with the media and content. Examples include discussing a map retrieved by GPS or participating in online games. These concurrent activities can be distracting, such as browsing two or three Web sites at the same time, or talking, eating, or checking e-mails while downloading Web content.

Post-exposure activities are related to short-term or long-term effects following the media exposure, for example, talking about someone's Facebook status, or being annoyed with spam or phishing e-mails that clutter your inbox. These post-exposure activities are closely related to gratification resulting from the media use.

The "Use" in U&G theory involves the specific choice of media type (e.g., mobile or PC) or channel (e.g., Yahoo! or Google). This choice largely depends on the habits or decisions made during the pre-exposure activity period and helps determine the degree of media exposure and audience involvement in during-exposure activity.

Finally, U&G theory identifies the types and degrees of gratification obtained from media exposure and determines how well they satisfy the original needs that initiated the media use process. The degree to which an individual obtains gratification through media use affects and reinforces future motives or gratification expectations.

U&G theory has been employed to identify online consumers' needs or motivations from fixed Internet on numerous occasions (Lin, 1999). Thus, it seems reasonable to assume it can also be applied to wireless Internet adoption. For example, Okazaki (2004) used a U&G paradigm and proposed three motivational antecedents of wireless pull advertising: entertainment, informativeness, and irritation. In a study on mobile e-mailing, Höflich and Rössler (2001) identified five gratifications: reassurance, sociability, immediate access/availability, instrumentality, and entertainment/enjoyment. In particular, immediate access/availability seems to be related to the ubiquitous nature of the device, as consumers may use mobile information at any time and any place, for example, while selecting products at stores or while window shopping, in order to make or modify their purchasing decision.

On the negative side of media usage, *perceived irritation* has been recognized as an influential factor in uses and gratifications studies of wired Internet usage: unsolicited, confusing information tends to annoy consumers. Consumers face a psychological dilemma in that accessing information may impose airtime and associated costs, but message content may be of real value. This is also the case with mobile communications. Consumers often feel disappointed with themselves when they are not capable of managing complex mobile devices to achieve their information needs. In addition, an implicit frustration may arise because of their potential loss of control over personal information, which can be disseminated without their knowledge or permission (Featherman & Pavlou, 2003).

Behavioral and attitudinal models

Researchers are increasingly interested in explicating why and how consumers adopt new technology. In particular, several theoretical models have been proposed in the area of psychology and information systems management. In this section, the most widely used behavioral and attitudinal models are explained.

Theory of reasoned action (TRA)

The theory of reasoned action (TRA; Ajzen & Fishbein, 1980; Fishbein & Ajzen, 1975) is one of the most important social psychological theories for predicting and understanding behavior. It was designed to model how any specific behavior under volitional control is produced by beliefs, attitude, and intention to perform that behavior. In this model, the formation of a behavioral intention is the immediate antecedent of action and mediates the influence of other variables on behavior (Fishbein & Ajzen, 1975). More specifically, intention is caused by both the individual's attitude toward performing that behavior and the social or normative beliefs about the appropriateness of the behavior. Fishbein and Ajzen (1975) identified the latter as a subjective norm. For example, one might have a very favorable attitude toward having a glass of wine during dinner at a restaurant. However, the intention to actually order a bottle of wine will be affected by the individual's beliefs about the appropriateness of ordering a bottle of wine in the present situation and the motivation to comply with those normative beliefs.

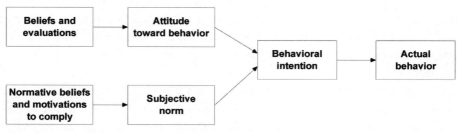

Fig. 2.4. Theory of Reasoned Action (TRA). Source: Fishbein and Ajzen (1975).

As another example, a consumer might have a very favorable attitude toward having a GPS function in his mobile device. However, the intention to actually use GPS will be influenced by the consumer's beliefs about the appropriateness of using the GPS in the current situation (e.g., finding a restaurant with friends for a fun meal or being lost while driving on a road in a foreign country) and his motivation to comply with those normative beliefs.

Ajzen and Fishbein's model has three important limitations. First, the model was developed to deal with behaviors (e.g., seeking a new house, applying for a consumer loan, taking a diet supplement) and not the outcomes of these behaviors (e.g., owning a new house, obtaining a consumer loan, or losing weight). The model concerns only those behaviors that are under a person's volitional control and thus cannot apply to actions determined (at least in part) by factors beyond his or her voluntary control. This is the case whenever the performance of some action demands knowledge, skills, resources, or cooperation from others or when the action should overcome environmental obstacles and the conditions of the model cannot be met. In such cases, the person may not be able to perform the action, even though the intention to do so is strong. For example, one may not be able to purchase a new house because the bank does not offer any mortgage loan or because the interest rate is unaffordable.

Second, TRA focuses on a single behavior and does not consider the possibility of choosing among alternative behaviors. Ajzen and Fishbein (1980) recognized that omitting the possibility of choosing among alternative behaviors was a serious limitation of the model. From consumer behavior perspectives, a "choice" is a constant issue in selecting stores, products, brands, models, contents, sizes, colors, and so on. Third, TRA's subjective norm covers only an injunctive social norm as opposed to descriptive social norms (Cialdini, Kallgren, & Reno, 1991; Sheeran & Taylor, 1999). Injunctive social norms explain the person's potential to gain approval or obtain sanction from significant others. In contrast, descriptive social norms relate to perceptions of significant others' attitudes and behaviors. The opinions and actions of significant others offer information that the person may use in deciding his or her action. TRA's subjective norm is only concerned with perceived social pressure to engage in a behavior. Descriptive social norms have been shown to influence intentions to engage in addictive behaviors such as smoking and gambling even when the effects of subjective norms have been controlled (Chassin, Presson, Sherman, & Edwards, 1991; Sheeran & Taylor, 1999). Research on social dilemmas and related mixed-motive conflicts have provided evidence that people often imitate the behavior of other participants in their group, due either to a "consensus heuristic" where others' behavior is used as a guideline in novel or ambiguous situations (Maheswaran & Chaiken, 1991), or to a "reciprocity rule" that is a central and powerful norm in social life (Hertel, Aarts, & Zeelenberg, 2002).

Technology acceptance model (TAM)

Fishbein and Ajzen's TRA appears to hold up quite well within the constraints they defined. However, later researchers became increasingly interested in the understanding and prediction of situations that do not fit neatly within Fishbein and Ajzen's framework. In particular, a model was needed to specifically address why people accept or reject information systems.

Shedding light on this question, Davis (1986, 1989) proposed the technology acceptance model (TAM), which quickly became one of the most frequently used models in IT research. TAM is one of the most influential adaptations of TRA, and it was specifically developed to predict individual adoption and use of new IT. TAM uses TRA as a theoretical basis but replaces many of TRA's attitude measures with two technology acceptance measures—*ease of use* (EOU) and *perceived usefulness* (PU). The central idea underlying TAM is that EOU and PU—not attitude—ultimately determine a person's behavioral intention to use an IT. PU refers to the extent to which a prospective user believes that using a specific IT will improve his or her job performance, while EOU refers to the extent to which a user expects the use of a specific IT to be relatively free of effort (Davis, 1986). Because effort is a finite resource that a person may allocate to the various activities for which he or she is responsible (Radner & Rothschild, 1975), TAM posits that—all else being equal—an application that is perceived to be easier to use than another is more likely to be accepted by users. In TAM, PU is seen as being directly impacted by EOU, with intention to use serving as a mediator of actual system use.

However, it should be noted that Davis and colleagues (1989) concluded that attitude did not appear to fully mediate the effect of perceived usefulness and perceived ease of use on behavioral intention as originally anticipated. It was therefore removed from the model. Thus, the original TAM proposed by Davis and his fellow researchers (1989) should be understood as the final model *without* attitude (Venkatesh & Davis, 1996).

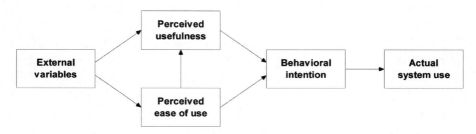

Fig. 2.5. Technology Acceptance Model. (TAM). Based on Davis (1989).

TAM has received extensive empirical support through validations, applications, and replications across a diverse range of information technology, including the mobile device (Barnes & Huff, 2003; Bruner & Kumar, 2005; Lu, Liu, & Yao, 2003; Luarn & Lin, 2005; Pagani, 2004; Whang & Chang, 2004; Wu & Wang, 2005). As a result, it is reported that TAM consistently explains approximately 40% of the variance in individuals' intention to use an IT and actual usage (Venkatesh & Bala, 2008).

In general, attempts to extend the TAM have taken one of three approaches: introducing factors from related models, introducing additional or alternative belief factors, and examining antecedents and moderators of perceived usefulness and perceived ease of use (Wixom & Todd, 2005). For example, Lu and colleagues (2005) argued that the TAM should include the influence of social/personal factors. Other scholars suggested integrating contingency variables into the TAM framework, including human factors, emotional factors, and social influence factors. Venkatesh and Davis (2000) maintained that research to date has not studied how perceived playfulness fits into the nomological network of a TAM. Venkatesh (2000) viewed anxiety as a determinant of process expectancy, such as perceived ease of use. Other scholars have proposed that computer playfulness and anxiety have significant effects on perceived ease of use. Lu and fellow researchers (2003) proposed social influences to predict perceived usefulness toward wireless Internet via mobile devices (WIMT) and concluded that social influence can promote and facilitate the acceptance of using WIMT.

In a context of online gaming adoption, Hsu and Lu (2004) added social influence and flow experience, which are conceptualized as antecedents of both attitude and intention. They found perceived ease of use to be the most important determinant of attitude, but perceived usefulness plays a minor role in this regard. In addition to flow experience, Ha and colleagues (2007) incorporated perceived enjoyment, perceived attractiveness, and perceived lower monetary sacrifice as antecedents of attitude. Their findings show that the effect of perceived enjoyment is the most solid, while perceived usefulness has no impact on attitude formation in a context of online gaming.

TAM2

One of the potential problems in the TAM was that it takes into account no social influence that individuals may receive from their external environment. This is precisely what Rogers (1995) postulated in his theory of diffusion of innovations. In addition, Thompson and colleagues (1991) stated that social influence factors, including norms (self-instructions to do what is perceived to be correct and appropriate by members of a culture in certain situations), roles (behaviors that are considered correct but relate to persons holding a particular position in a group, society, or social system), and values (abstract categories with strong affective components) could strongly affect intention and behavior. Thus, it seems reasonable to incorporate not only intrinsic motivation factors but also factors of social influence into the TAM model.

Based on this, Venkatesh and Davis (2000) proposed TAM2 by identifying and theorizing about the general determinants of perceived usefulness, which can be broadly categorized into two groups: social influence and system characteristics. Social influence is characterized by subjective norm and image. System characteristics comprise job relevance, output quality, result demonstrability, and perceived ease of use. In addition, as shown in Figure 2.6, TAM2 proposes two moderators: experience and voluntariness. Subjective norm can be defined as a "person's perception that most people who are important to him think he should or should not perform the behavior in question" (Fishbein & Ajzen, 1975, p. 302). As with TRA, subjective norm is also conceptualized as a direct determinant of behavioral intention. The rationale for a direct effect of subjective norm on intention is that people may behave a certain way, even if they do not particularly favor the behavior or its consequences, if they believe "one or more important referents think they should, and they are sufficiently motivated to comply with the referents" (Venkatesh & Davis, 2000, p. 187). In TAM2, the subjective norm also has an *indirect* effect on the behavioral intention through PU and PEOU (i.e., mediation). This "*internalization process*" represents the tendency of people to take the opinions of others as truth..

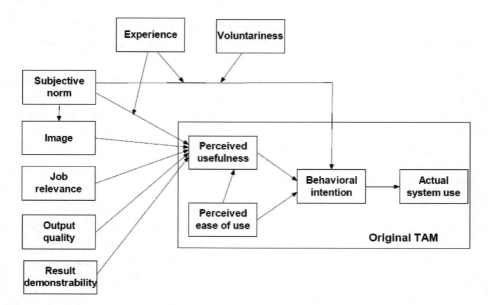

Fig. 2.6. TAM2. Source: Venkatesh and Davis (2000).

In addition, TAM2 uses four constructs—job relevance, output quality, result demonstrability, and perceived ease of use—to capture the influence of cognitive instrumental processes on perceived usefulness. Drawing on three different theoretical frameworks—work motivation theory (e.g., Vroom, 1982), action identification theory (e.g., Vallacher & Wegner, 1987), and behavioral decision theory (e.g., Beach & Mitchell, 1998)—Venkatesh and Davis (2000) provided a detailed discussion of how and why individuals form perceptions of usefulness based on cognitive instrumental processes. The core theoretical argument underlying the role of cognitive instrumental processes is that individuals "form perceived usefulness judgment in part by cognitively comparing what a system is capable of doing with what they need to get done in their job" (Venkatesh & Davis, 2000, p. 190). TAM2 posits that individuals' perceptions of how well their work objectives coincide with the perceived benefits of using the system in question to ultimately form the basis of how they judge the usefulness of the system (Venkatesh & Davis, 2000).

TAM3

Venkatesh (2000) developed a model of the determinants of perceived ease of use based on the notion that individuals will predetermine a system's ease of use through their predisposition toward computers and their use. These pre-existing beliefs include *computer self-efficacy, computer anxiety,* and *computer playfulness;* and *perceptions of external control* (or *facilitating conditions*). Venkatesh and Bala (2008) incorporated these determinants of perceived ease of use into TAM2 (Venkatesh & Davis, 2000) and developed the TAM3 model.

As Figure 2.7 illustrates, TAM3 proposes that experience will play a part in the following interactions: (1) the relationship between perceived ease of use and perceived usefulness; (2) the relationship between computer anxiety and perceived ease of use; and (3) the relationship between perceived ease of use and behavioral intention. These causal relationships were not empirically tested by Venkatesh (2000) or Venkatesh and Davis (2000).

Theory of planned behavior (TPB)

Another widely used extension of the TRA is the theory of planned behavior (TPB) (Ajzen, 1991). This model has been employed extensively to predict consumer acceptance of information technology (e.g., Venkatesh et al., 2003; Wu & Wang, 2005). The TPB states that behavioral intentions are determined by three primary dimensions: attitude, subjective norm, and perceived behavioral control. All three factors are influenced by a set of cognitive beliefs about the innovation and their respective importance, described as an expectancy-value formula.

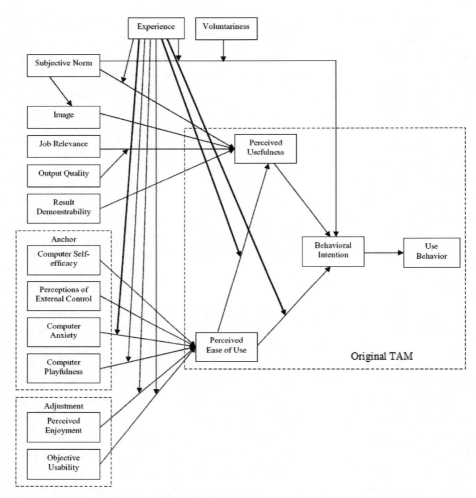

Fig. 2.7. TAM3. Source: Venkatesh and Bala (2008).

Perceived behavioral control can be defined as *"a person's perception of how easy or difficult it would be to carry out a behavior"* (Ajzen, 1991). The concept is similar to Bandura's (1982) concept of self-efficacy. Here, control is seen as a continuum with easily executed behaviors at one end (e.g., brushing one's teeth) and behavioral goals demanding resources, opportunities, and specialized skills (e.g., becoming a world-class chess player) at the other. The link between intentions and behavior reflects the fact that people tend to engage in behaviors they intend to perform. Perceived behavioral control not only influences the intention to perform a certain behavior but also has a direct effect on actual behavior. However, the link between perceived behavioral control and behavior is more complex. This relationship suggests that we are more likely to engage in (attractive/desirable) behaviors we have control over. It also suggests that we are prevented from carrying out behaviors over which we have no control. Conversely, it suggests that if intentions are held constant, behavior will more likely be performed as perceived behavioral control increases.

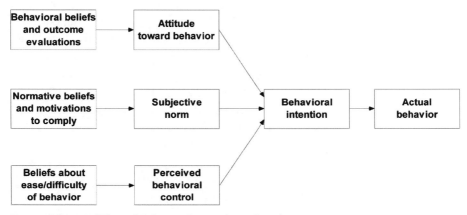

Fig. 2.8. Theory of Planned Behavior. Source: Ajzen (1991).

Ajzen (1991) argues that, because performance of a behavior is a joint function of intentions and perceived behavioral control, several conditions have to be met for accurate prediction. First, the measures of intention and perceived behavioral control must correspond to (Ajzen & Fishbein, 1980) or be compatible with (Ajzen, 1991) the behavior that is to be predicted. That is, intentions and perceptions of control must be assessed in relation to the particular behavior of interest, and the specified context must be the same as that in which the behavior is to occur. For example, if the behavior to be predicted is adopting mobile Internet services, then we must assess intentions to adopt mobile Internet services, not intentions to use a mobile phone in general, or intentions to access the Internet in personal computers.

By the same token, perceived control over adopting mobile Internet services should be assessed. The second condition for accurate behavioral prediction is that intentions and perceived behavioral control must remain stable in the interval between their assessment and the observation of the behavior. Intervening events may produce changes in intentions or in perceptions of behavioral control, with the result that the original measures of these variables may no longer permit accurate prediction of behavior. The third requirement for predictive validity has to do with the accuracy of perceived behavioral control, because prediction of behavior from perceived behavioral control should improve to the extent that perceptions of behavioral control realistically reflect actual control.

The TPB is regarded as an inclusive behavior theory due to the fact that outside influences on behavior are illustrated as just that—components outside the scope of the model. In this regard, the TPB may be better understood as a theory that incorporates proximal determinants of behavior. The model adequately describes the processes by which attitudes and beliefs determine behavior but not the process by which other variables (e.g., personality) influence components of the TPB. Meta-analytic reviews of the TPB provide strong support for the predictive validity of the TPB in terms of the percentage of variance explained in behavior and intentions by the components of the TPB (Godin & Kok, 1996; Sutton, 1998).

Despite its merits, prior research pointed out two potential problems with TPB. First, it is assumed that a person may possess a large number of beliefs about a particular behavior, but that at any one time only some of these are likely to be salient. It is the salient beliefs that are assumed to determine a person's attitude. However, it is not a simple matter to ascertain which beliefs are salient (Ajzen, Nichols, & Driver, 1995). Second, the TPB is primarily concerned with individuals' beliefs. The supplying of beliefs by researchers may not adequately capture the beliefs salient to the individual, no matter how extensive the pilot works.

Decomposed TPB (or Combined TAM and TPB)

Taylor and Todd (1995) introduced the so-called "decomposed TPB," which draws upon constructs from the innovations-characteristics literature. This model pretends to more completely explore the dimensions of attitudinal, normative, and control beliefs into multidimensional belief constructs. Specifically, this model incorporates additional factors, such as the influence of significant others, perceived ability, and control that were not taken into account in TAM but have proven to be important determinants of IT usage behavior (Ajzen, 1991).

Attitudinal belief dimensions were derived from the perceived characteristics of an innovation conceptualized by Rogers (1976): relative advantage, complexity, and compatibility. These dimensions have been used in a direct or indirect way in prior research on computer technology adoption. *Relative advantage* refers to "the degree to which an innovation provides benefits which supersede those of its precursor and may incorporate factors such as economic benefits, image enhancement, convenience and satisfaction" (Rogers, 1976) and is analogous to the perceived usefulness (PU) in TAM. *Complexity* represents "the degree to which an innovation is perceived to be difficult to understand, learn or operate" (Rogers,

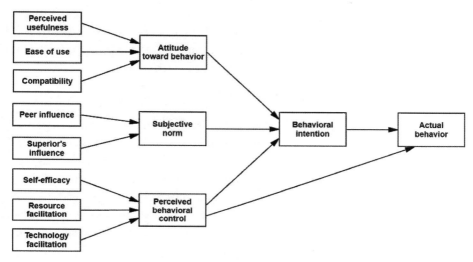

Fig. 2.9. Decomposed TPB. Source: Taylor and Todd (1995).

1976). *Compatibility* represents "the degree to which an innovation fits with the potential adopter's existing values, previous experiences and current needs" (Rogers, 1976).

Normative belief structure was decomposed into three important referent groups in an organizational setting: peers, superiors, and subordinates. Each referent group may share very different opinions on the new computer technology. For example, one's superiors may view the use of the new technology favorably because it would increase productivity. On the other hand, one's peers may be reluctant to adopt the new technology because it demands too much change in their routine work. In the end, the effects of superiors and peers may cancel each other out, thus producing no influence on subjective norm. Taylor and Todd (1995) used only peers and superiors in their model.

For perceived control, Taylor and Todd (1995) followed Ajzen's (1991) conceptualization and included the internal notion of individual "self-efficacy" and external resource constraints, or "facilitating conditions." The social cognitive theory of self-efficacy has been useful in understanding individuals' behavior and performance in a variety of activities (Venkatesh & Davis, 1996). Self-efficacy provides important implications for several issues related to organizational behavior and human resource management, including selection, leadership training, vocational counseling, locus of control, equal employment opportunity, performance appraisals, goals, and incentives. One of the important causes of self-efficacy is one's own experience in a situation or similar situation. The observation of a similar task performed by some other person could also nurture self-efficacy beliefs. Self-efficacy is also strongly related to future performance, and prior research finds that self-efficacy tailored to a computer or information technology context is an important determinant of the perceptions of users about such technologies.

Unified Theory of Acceptance and Use of Technology (UTAUT)

As we have seen, Venkatesh and Davis (2000) attempted to introduce an extension to TAM and TAM2 that examined the influences of select antecedent social influence and cognitive instrumental constructs on perceived usefulness and usage intentions. Later, Venkatesh and others (2003) synthesized eight models of technology acceptance into the Unified Theory of Acceptance and Use of Technology (UTAUT). UTAUT seems to represent a significant step forward from its predecessors, and it suggests four core constructs to explain and predict user acceptance of a new technology: performance expectancy (equivalent to perceived usefulness), effort expectancy (equivalent to perceived ease of use), facilitating conditions, and social influence. These constructs explain up to 70% of the variance in usage intention.

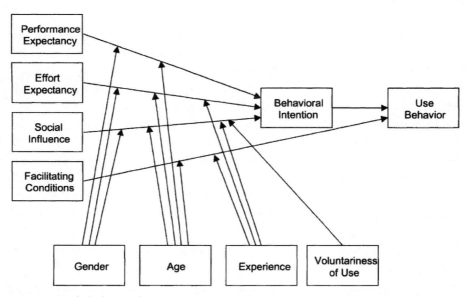

Fig. 2.10. Unified Theory of Acceptance and Use of Technology (UTAUT). Source: Venkatesh et al. (2003).

Expectation-Disconfirmation model (EDM)

The Expectation-Disconfirmation model (EDM) was originally developed by Oliver (1980), who theorized that consumers' product repurchase or reuse is determined by their satisfaction with prior experience. The primary argument of EDM is that, while initial acceptance of a new product is an important first step, long-term viability of the product and its eventual success depend on its continued use rather than first-time use. In this model, consumers form their initial expectation of a specific product or service prior to purchase. Second, they accept and use that product or service. Following a period of initial consumption, they form perceptions about its performance. Third, they assess its perceived performance vis-à-vis their original expectation and determine the extent to which their expectation is confirmed (disconfirmation). It follows that low expectations and high product performance result in greater confirmation. This causes consumers to be more satisfied and therefore promotes product repurchase or reuse. The opposite is also true: high expectations and low product performance cause disconfirmation, dissatisfaction, and discontinued use. As Figure 2.11 shows, confirmation is inversely related to expectation and directly related to perceived performance. The fourth step by consumers is to determine their level of satisfaction. This is based on their expectation level and subsequently on their confirmation level. The final step of this process is the determination of repurchase intention: satisfied consumers continue to use the products in question, while dissatisfied users discontinue their use.

Based on the previous discussion, EDT predicts that the decision to repurchase a product or service is determined primarily by consumers' satisfaction with a prior experience with that product or service (Oliver, 1980). Thus, satisfaction is viewed as the key to building and retaining a loyal base of long-term consumers (Anderson & Sullivan, 1993, p. 160). The EDT also posits expectation as an additional determinant of satisfaction, in that expectation acts as a reference point for consumers to make evaluative judgments about the product or service in question.

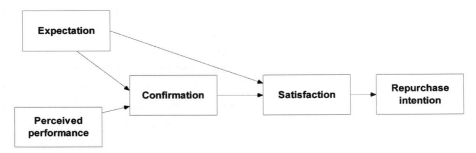

Fig. 2.11. Expectation-Disconfirmation Model (EDM). Source: Based on Oliver (1980).

Comparison of predictive power

Numerous studies have attempted to test the predictive power of these models. The literature suggests that TAM receives the most empirical support in information technology research. For example, Davis, Bagozzi, and Warshaw (1989) compared TAM and TRA in the prediction of software usage intention and found that the former outperformed the latter. In Mathieson's (1991) study, TAM predicted intention to use a spreadsheet package better than did TPB. Hong, Thong, and Tam (2006) compared TAM with two variations of the Expectation-Confirmation Model (ECM) proposed by Bhattacherjee (2001) for continued mobile Internet usage. Drawn upon the consumer behavior literature, ECM holds that consumers' intention to repurchase a product or continue use of a service is determined primarily by their satisfaction in prior use of that product or service (Anderson & Sullivan, 1993). Satisfaction is viewed as the key to building and retaining a loyal base of long-term consumers: "Investing in customer satisfaction is like taking out an insurance policy" (Bhattacherjee, 2001). ECM also posits expectation as an additional determinant of satisfaction, in that expectation acts as a reference point for consumers to make evaluative judgments about the focal product or service. However, the authors found that TAM performed better than ECM and its extended variation in terms of its parsimony and flexibility, concluding that TAM provides researchers with a quick, relatively easy, and inexpensive way of conducting research on users' post-adoption behavior. Furthermore, although TAM was originally designed to understand users' behavior at the initial stage of IT adoption, it can be extended to the understanding of continued usage behavior of experienced users. However, a thorough comparison of the above-mentioned models in terms of their predictive power is far beyond the scope of this chapter. We encourage readers to conduct a brief review of e- or m-commerce research that adopts or extends these models.

To date, much research on the mobile Internet has adopted one or a combination of the models described in this chapter. Lu, Liu, and Yao (2003) proposed a TAM-based conceptual framework for wireless Internet adoption. Hung, Ku, and Chang (2003) carried out one of the first empirical explorations in that the authors attempted to investigate WAP service adoption in terms of TPB and IDT. To date, Nysveen, Pedersen, and Thorbjornsen's study (2005) is one of the most cited in mobile commerce research. The study was carried out in Norway and attempted to validate a causal model based on the TAM, TRA, and TPB. It also examined cross-service comparisons via multigroup structural equation modeling. Other extensions of the behavioral models can be found in mobile gaming adoption

(Okazaki, Skapa, & Grande, 2008), mobile coupon redemption (Dickinger & Kleijnen, 2008), and mobile advertising (Muk, 2007; Kim, Park, & Oh, 2008; and Zhang & Mao, 2008), among others.

Summary

A theory is the language that allows scholars to move from observation to observation and make sense of similarities and differences. We need a solid and consistent theoretical framework to interpret and understand the complex phenomenon of mobile marketing. This chapter starts with the general conceptualization of innovation diffusion, adoption motives, and social influence, based on the diffusion of innovations theory (Rogers, 1976) and the uses and gratifications theory (Lin, 1999). Then the chapter explicates behavioral and attitudinal models that have been used in new technology adoption. This section begins with two of the most widely used models, theory of reasoned action (TRA) and technology adoption model (TAM). It then extends the description to TAM2, TAM3, theory of planned behavior (TPB), decomposed TPB, Unified Theory of Acceptance and Use of Technology (UTAUT), and expectation-disconfirmation model (EDM). In mobile marketing research, these theoretical models have been widely used and extended.

3

Mobile Marketing Framework

While mobile marketing is increasingly popular, it is misleading to overemphasize its role in firms' holistic marketing. Mobile marketing should be integrated or combined as a tool to create an effective customer acquisition program. Especially popular is the use of mobile marketing in customer loyalty programs. These are programs sponsored by a firm to encourage repeat purchases through program enrollment processes and the distribution of awards, discount coupons, and so on. Firms could send an SMS or print QR codes in promotional leaflets for upcoming events or sales, expecting customers to redeem such benefits. Airlines, retail stores, and consumer goods manufacturers are already engaged in the use of such mobile-based promotion. In this light, mobile marketing is more effective in the short term rather than the long term. However, looking into each individual case may lead to an erroneous view of mobile marketing and losing sight of the big picture. In the past few years, the mobile marketing landscape has begun to open up a whole new realm of possibilities for marketers and advertisers.

This chapter establishes our conceptual base for mobile marketing. It is based on an increasingly important topic in information systems but one that is somewhat neglected in marketing: cloud computing. In what follows, we first explain what cloud computing consists of and how this concept can be adapted in a marketing concept. Our intention is *not* to adopt cloud computing as it is used in computer science, but to export the idea into our holistic mobile marketing framework. On this basis, our mobile marketing model is introduced. According to this model, we describe five stages of consumer decision making from mobile marketing perspectives.

Marketing based on cloud computing

It makes little sense to try to conceptualize mobile marketing from traditional perspectives—strategic and tactical planning, segmentation, targeting, and positioning, among others—without taking into account a key concept underlying our new e-commerce era: cloud computing. Broadly defined, cloud computing is the creation of Internet-related value, irrespective of the use of downloadable applications or Web-based services (Kobayashi, 2010). It serves as a main idea guiding the transition from PC-based information processing to Web-based information processing. Opinions vary regarding the definition of cloud computing, but experts unanimously acknowledge the importance of this concept for the forthcoming era. Following are six definitions of cloud computing by industry experts.

> For me the simplest explanation for cloud computing is describing it as, "internet centric software." This new cloud computing software model is a shift from the traditional single tenant approach to software development to that of a scalable, multi-tenant, multi-platform, multi-network, and global. This could be as simple as your web based email service or as complex as a globally distributed load balanced content delivery environment....As software transitions from a traditional desktop deployment model to that of a network & data centric one, 'the cloud' will be the key way in which you develop, deploy and manage applications in this new computing paradigm.
>
> —REUVEN COHEN, FOUNDER & CTO, ENOMALY INC.

> I view cloud computing as a broad array of web-based services aimed at allowing users to obtain a wide range of functional capabilities on a "pay-as-you-go" basis that previously required tremendous hardware/software investments and professional skills to acquire. Cloud computing is the realization of the earlier ideals of utility computing without the technical complexities or complicated deployment worries.
>
> —JEFF KAPLAN, MANAGING DIRECTOR, THINKSTRATEGIES.

People are coming to grips with Virtualization and how it reshapes IT, creates service and software based models, and in many ways changes a lot of the physical layer we are used to. Clouds will be the next transformation over the next several years, building off of the software models that virtualization enabled.

—Douglas Gourlay, Vice President of Marketing, Arista Networks.

The way I understand it, "cloud computing" refers to the bigger picture...basically the broad concept of using the internet to allow people to access technology-enabled services. According to Gartner, those services must be "massively scalable" to qualify as true "cloud computing." So according to that definition, every time I log into Facebook, or search for flights online, I am taking advantage of cloud computing....The "Cloud" concept is finally wrapping peoples' minds around what is possible when you leverage web-scale infrastructure (application and physical) in an on-demand way. "Managed Services," "ASP," "Grid Computing," "Software as a Service," "Platform as a Service," "Anything as a Service"....all terms that couldn't get it done. Call it a "Cloud" and everyone goes bonkers. Go figure.

—Damon Edwards, CEO, DTO Solutions.

The "cloud" model initially has focused on making the hardware layer consumable as on-demand compute and storage capacity. This is an important first step, but for companies to harness the power of the cloud, complete application infrastructure needs to be easily configured, deployed, dynamically-scaled and managed in these virtualized hardware environments.

—Kirill Sheynkman, Venture Partner at Greycroft Partners.

Cloud computing overlaps some of the concepts of distributed, grid and utility computing, however it does have its own meaning if contextually used correctly. Cloud computing really is accessing resources and services needed to perform functions with dynamically changing needs. An application or service developer requests access from the cloud rather than a specific endpoint or named resource. What goes on in the cloud manages multiple infrastructures across multiple organizations and consists of one or more frameworks overlaid on top of the infrastructures tying them together. The cloud is a virtualization of resources that maintains and manages itself.

—Kevin Hartig, Sun Microsystems.

Source: Based on Geelan (2009)

Using this concept, the computing infrastructure converts itself into a cloud from which businesses and users are able to access applications from anywhere in the world, on demand. Thus, our attention will no longer be geared toward our individual computers, but toward data content across the Internet without reference to the underlying hosting infrastructure. This idea is a drastic departure from locally installed programs to an invisible platform where all information is stored and controlled upon demand. For example, when you purchase a new Android phone, you do not have to set up a new Gmail account. Instead, you can access an existing Gmail account by logging in with your account name and password, because Gmail data are stored in Google servers. Similarly, when you create a spreadsheet with the Google Docs service, major components of the software reside on unseen computers, whereabouts unknown, possibly scattered across continents. By the same token, iPhone is broadly supported by iTunes and the App Store with a diverse range of music, videos, and applications, all of which are stored in a data center. In fact, Apple furthered this eco-system concept into iCloud, which is based on cloud computing. iCloud remembers your device's settings, apps, home screen layouts, ringtones, and text messages, so all of that information is available if you upgrade or replace your iPhone or iPad (PCWorld, 2011). Table 3.1 lists 10 primary benefits of cloud computing.

From a marketing point of view, cloud computing can be paraphrased as multi-device marketing in which consumers can access the same information through a diverse range of terminals, including PC, smartphone, tablet, or e-book. Husson (2011), a principal analyst with Forrester Research serving consumer product strategy professionals, argues that a new era has opened when marketers and advertisers need a new cross-platform approach to loyalty. He writes:

> While we expect browsers and apps to coexist on tablets and smartphones in the next three to five years, the rise of the application era will have implications for existing business models and will open up new opportunities. Mobile services will be one of many customer touchpoints. App innovation started on smartphones, but the concept of app stores will expand to other increasingly connected devices and platforms. Apps will become touchpoints for content services. They will have to work across all platforms—including mobile, TV, and the PC. No matter what the technology used—be it a traditional Internet website on a PC or a mobile app on a mobile device—consumers will expect a seamless, cross-channel user experience. The service will have to be contextualized depending on the device's form factor and the location from which the user is using her connected device.

TABLE 3.1. Key Benefits of Cloud Computing

Key benefits	Description
Efficient use of IT resources	On-premise software requires that each individual workstation be installed with software that must also be legally licensed to that workstation. The software functions independently of other workstations, as does its maintenance. This requires time, energy, and cost, as businesses have had to hire IT staff and even, depending on the business's size, entire IT departments to ensure that each workstation's software is maintained and functioning properly. With cloud computing solutions, the software is Web-based, and requires only Internet access and a Web browser.
Easy storage and maintenance	Not only does the Web-based software not require any installation or IT maintenance within a business, but the responsibility of storing, maintaining, and processing the information on the software is outside of the company. Any glitches or malfunctions, should there be any, are handled elsewhere—remotely, on the cloud—meaning that the business need not be concerned with such problems.
Enhanced internal communications	With on-premise software, data may be stored in one or more computers, and often requires manual entry and tedious communication efforts. The margin for miscommunication error is, thus, quite large. With a Web-based software solution, all the business executives and employees interact with the same interface that reflects the same data. Everyone, once logged in, can view the same information, ensuring consistency and improving internal communications greatly.
Accurate, real-time information	Web-based solutions focused on customer relationship management (CRM) track, store, and monitor all the activity of individual customers; but perhaps even more significantly, it is done in real time. This means that any permitted employee or executive can retrieve data on demand and compile reports that accurately reflect the most up-to-the-minute information.
Sales support	By having accurate, up-to-the-minute data, sales and marketing departments have readily available information with which to more rapidly begin formulating sales and marketing strategies.

TABLE 3.1. (*continued*)

Key benefits	Description
Accurate customer data	Because the marketing department has access to accurate and current information, this information can be easily analyzed, and opportunities for growth are available through using sales strategies that are specifically tailored to meet the specific needs and interests of different customers.
Customer relationship management	Since sales and marketing initiatives can be better tailored to specific customers, and since those customers are allowed the opportunity to personalize their buying exchanges with the business, this wholly improves customer relationship management, which is crucial to a business's success in today's marketplace.
Resource management	Cutting out the administrative work associated with manually keeping information current can allow for time being spent elsewhere, such as tracking sales leads.
Better business tracking	The ninth benefit of implementing cloud computing solutions in a business is the ability for top executives, partners, and/or company heads to carefully monitor the business's profitability, with more accuracy and up-to-the-minute information.
Costs	Businesses find that cloud computing solutions ultimately cut costs. Costs are cut in data entry, customer service call centers, IT departments, and marketing research.

Source: Based on Cloud Computing World (2011)

This cloud computing serves as a strategic turning point for mobile marketers and advertisers, since individual terminals are no longer a focal point of debate. In other words, the execution (and effectiveness) of mobile marketing will no longer depend on the device itself. Under cloud-based mobile marketing, firms' marketing efforts should shift from "how to target customers" to "how to give them access." Here, the only objective firms need to achieve is to create holistic or integrated marketing programs that can be implemented and accessed by multiple devices, including mobile devices. In other words, no single marketing program needs to be tailor-made for mobile devices. Instead, firms develop, upload, and control their marketing programs into a cloud, from which distinct terminals can access a broad array of Web-based resources, including PC, mobile device, tablet, netbook, and e-book readers, among others. For example, search engines, consumer review sites, or SNS can be programmed and controlled on the cloud, which consumers could access from any Internet terminal. GPS-based programs can be configured on the cloud so that all geographic information can be stored and retrieved later from any other media. In a way, cloud computing makes marketers and advertisers truly centralize, integrate, and coordinate all necessary marketing programs, without reference to the type of endpoints.

Figure 3.1 presents the basic concept of cloud-based marketing. Within the cloud, firms could configure the contents for marketing mix, applications, and clients' database (personal data). The cloud-based marketing model enables marketers and advertisers to increase capacity or add a diverse range of capabilities without investing in new infrastructure, training new personnel, or licensing new software. Cloud computing encompasses any subscription-based or pay-per-use service that, in real time over the Internet, extends IT's existing capabilities. In this way, marketing mix variables can be delivered through Web-based applications via the browser to thousands of customers using a multi-device strategy. However, in this model, the services may not necessarily be outsourced using existing or commercially available services such as Google Apps or iCloud. Mobile Marketing in Action 3.1 describes how McDonald's sees cloud computing as a way to cut costs and enhance flexibility.

According to a new Forrester report called "Sizing the Cloud," the global cloud computing market is expected to reach US$241 billion in 2020, compared to US$40.7 billion in 2010. The report provides market forecasts on 12 different market segments for the next decade, forecasting shifts in the usage patterns of cloud infrastructure, business applications for the cloud, and cloud platforms that are becoming increasingly widespread. According to "Sizing the Cloud", Software-as-a-Service (SaaS) offers more growth opportunity than any other segment in the still vaguely defined market for cloud computing services. The report also predicts that SaaS will retain its position as a leading segment in cloud computing, with the SaaS market growing threefold to $92.8 billion by 2016. In contrast, Infrastructure-as-a-Service (IaaS) will witness rapid growth in the next few years, but Forrester expects dynamic infrastructure services to perform better than IaaS in the long term (Cloud Tweaks, 2011).

In this light, there are three technical breakthroughs that industry leaders have been struggling to achieve. First, the World Wide Web Consortium (W3C) has been moving forward to develop next-generation Web standards, "HTML5." W3C standards define "an Open Web Platform for application development that has the unprecedented potential to enable developers to build rich interactive experiences, powered by vast data stores, which are available on any device"

Fig. 3.1. Cloud-Based Marketing.
Note: Cloud computing has tremendously impacted businesses. Not only does cloud computing present the opportunity for businesses to improve efficiency without having to deal with on-premise software, but it also presents substantially advantageous opportunities for sales and marketing initiatives. Source: Own elaboration.

(W3C, 2011). Second, HTML5 is the next version of the Hyper Text Markup Language, a platform-neutral standard used worldwide for rendering Web pages. Apple, Google, and Microsoft touted the still-unfinished standard as the basis for building Web applications. For example, in August 2011, Google (2011) announced offline access to Gmail, Calendar, and Docs through its HTML5-based Chrome Web application. Similarly, the latest version of Apple's Safari Web browser on iOS 4.2 can be used for every iPhone, iPod, or iPad device and provides some major changes in HTML5 support, such as WebSocket[1] and Accelerometer support,[2] print support, new JavaScript data-types, and better SVG[3] support (Apple, 2011a). Third, the standardization of JavaScript enables firms to develop cross-platform applications. Web applications are basically those characterized by rich user experiences and interfaces (often involving JavaScript, HTML, Flash, etc.) and Web-service architectures with social interactions. Because Internet access is not necessarily continuous, many Web applications are used in an offline form. Thus, our thumbs have come to enjoy playing with offline versions of these Web Apps for our smartphones or "native apps," which have been creating problems for Web developers. While native apps and mobile devices fit nicely into our busy daily lives, these types of applications are hardly device independent, and thus multiple different versions of their native apps must be created for different mobile operating systems: iPhone, iPad, and Mac native apps are developed in Objective-C/Cocoa; native apps for Windows and Windows Mobile are written in C#/.NET; and many cross-platform apps and mobile apps for Android are written in Java. The biggest potential benefit of HTML5 is, therefore, its capacity that allows app developers to focus on making one version of each app (InfoWorld, 2011).

Nonetheless, despite the enormous potential of cloud computing, it seems necessary to recognize its potential drawbacks in order to make our discussion more objective. Despite its cost effectiveness, consumers need to assume an immense social cost, threatening the privacy and freedom of people who are too willing to trade it away for perceived convenience (The Drum, 2011). Furthermore, an over-reliance on cloud computing can blind us to the danger related to server unavailability and account lockout in "the cloud we rely on" caused by a cloud service provider—this is more likely to cause a service disruption than a hacker hacking the clouds (Lifehacker, 2009). For example, in September 2009, Google's Gmail online e-mail system was crashed worldwide due to on a traffic jam on its servers, leaving many users without access to their e-mail for nearly two hours (Paul, 2009). This incident would cast doubt on such over-dependence on cloud computing, especially for those users who had no email backups in their hard disks. According to two separate studies in 2007 (Carnegie Mellon University and Google), anywhere from 2 to 13 percent of all hard drives will fail in a given year. However, such a hard drive failure would affect a much smaller number of users in comparison to a cloud outage that could affect millions of people all over the world. Still, many people still believe in Google's reliability and trust that their data will always be there (Paul, 2009).

MOBILE MARKETING IN ACTION 3.1

Moving to the Cloud: A "Rational" Choice for McDonald's

When Scott Farnum of McDonald's saw the opportunity to move the fast-food chain's application-development tooling environment to the cloud, he did not hesitate.

Farnum, who is global infrastructure lab manager for McDonald's Corp. and is responsible for the company's application-development strategy, saw the cloud as a way to cut costs and enhance flexibility for his development teams, which have standardized on the IBM Rational toolset.

Like many other companies contemplating moving parts of their business to a cloud-computing environment, Farnum and his team weighed many factors, including the amount of downtime the company's developers have between projects.

The decision to move to the cloud made sense, considering the nature of application development with McDonald's IT department.

"There are several months where we do very little development, and then there are several months where things are very busy," Farnum said. "So the challenge for me is when I'm trying to provide an environment for my application teams to deliver a product and they need XYZ tooling, I have to buy enough tooling to cover everyone in that peak moment, which ends up being really costly.

"Then, outside that peak moment, we are not using those tools, and in some cases we will slow down development accordingly," he continued. "So we needed a model that was going to be flexible to any business condition and any development condition. Sometimes, we have big development years, and sometimes we have big deployment years. We needed this model to be flexible enough to handle that and go from there."

Once the decision to move McDonald's application-development needs to the cloud was set, the company tapped IBM partner CloudOne.

CloudOne specializes in taking IBM's Rational toolset to the cloud, and that is all the company does, said CloudOne CEO John McDonald, who spoke to eWEEK during IBM Innovate 2011, IBM's annual conference for Rational users.

CloudOne's Rational expertise is critical for Farnum since McDonald's uses Rational legacy tools, including ClearCase, ClearQuest and RequisitePro. The company is also evaluating Rational's newer tools, such as Rational Software Architect, Rational Application Developer and Rational Asset Manager.

More importantly, with the CloudOne solution, McDonald's can pay only for what it needs when it needs it.

Farnum chose Rational because McDonald's required tools that cover the entire software-development lifecycle and have a particular focus on application-lifecycle management. He also said an independent study by McDonald's found that the Rational toolset was "best of breed" and had the best opportunity to go "end-to-end"—from requirements to deployment to maintenance.

"Flexibility and elasticity are the key words here," said David Locke, director of worldwide marketing strategy for the cloud at IBM Rational.

However, being best-in-class comes with a price. The Rational toolset is not inexpensive, which made the cloud option even more attractive.

"McDonald's is a hamburger company; we don't want to be in the IT business," Farnum said. "We want to focus on what we do best. And we are always on the look-out for firms to come in and provide consulting services on their respective technologies to help us do what we need to do from a business perspective."

CloudOne was in a unique position in that it had begun providing consulting services to McDonald's in a different capacity. CloudOne then offered a cloud-computing solution to McDonald's, and Farnum jumped at the opportunity.

"At the time, we could not find another supplier that provided this and was able to also provide the SAAS [software as a service] model that we needed," he said.

From an implementation perspective, to prepare for the cloud, Farnum said IT managers need to be in the most flexible mode prior to going to the cloud, such as having primarily Web-based systems. "So, in our environment, we are leveraging CCRC [ClearCase Remote Client] as much as possible," he said.

Since moving to the cloud, McDonald's has seen "huge benefits," Farnum said.

For instance, the company has gotten a 50 percent improvement in the performance of the products.

"When we went to CloudOne, it became easier for them to support the products if they siloed each one onto its own server set," he said.

"That sped all those applications up, and made them easier to support," Farnum added. "And we could do things like upgrade that one product for Windows 7 if we needed to and leave the others alone. Other benefits are easier pilots. I'm not dependent on internal infrastructure folks to spin up a box and grant me administrative rights.

"I don't have to worry about all these aspects that go into a pilot or proof-of-concept. And, frankly, if we wanted to do a six-month pilot instead of a 30-day pilot, we have that flexibility. We can even do a pay-as-you-go pilot if we need to, because it's that flexible," Farnum explains.

Meanwhile, CloudOne's McDonald said the capital cost of getting into the Rational tools is prohibitive for many companies. The infrastructure to run the toolset and the people to set it up, monitor it and maintain it is beyond the reach of many companies.

An example of this is a customer that has a project requiring 20 people on it, but the company only owns 10 licenses. At this point, a company's options are limited.

The IT department and development teams either have to pony up the money for the extra licenses, cut costs in other areas, or change tools and maybe go with an open-source technology that is less expensive from an up-front cost level. But with CloudOne, they have another option that lets them use what they want but only pay for what they use, McDonald said.

"What we do at CloudOne is we offer up a way they can literally get into this with no money down," McDonald said. "We lower the transom of entry to zero, and it allows people who may not otherwise be able to use Rational tools or use as many Rational tools as they want to be able to do that."

Source: Taft (2011)

Mobile marketing model

Keeping cloud computing in mind as a key background, let's turn our attention to our mobile marketing model. Among the various options of Internet access, the mobile device is especially suited to personalizing any marketing actions according to time and location flexibility. In fact, ubiquity is the very unique characteristic of this channel, since no other media could capture moving targets as efficiently as a mobile device, irrespective of time and space. However, my impression is that this ubiquitous nature has often been overemphasized as a special capability that enables marketers and advertisers to offer "tailor-made" services. This is true, but it seems that more important is the capability of accessing the same database as other access terminals from cloud computing perspectives. In this regard, although mobile marketing has its historical roots in direct marketing, it is moving toward a more complex concept. Mobile marketing should be understood as an alternative channel for delivering the same content and applications as the other terminals can, but in a ubiquitous way. For example, the same advertising content can be sent and viewed with either a PC or a smartphone. Mobile couponing and payment are feasible with either PC or mobile, so that retailers can be more competitive by offering alternative payment methods and reduced prices, depending upon the location. In terms of product, a mobile site could foster familiarity and awareness of brand in a different format (i.e., size and layout), but the delivered information should be the same.

Our mobile marketing model combines three principal axes: (1) cloud-based 4Ps (marketing mix); (2) consumer decision process (hereafter CD process), which is typically used in consumer behavior (Blackwell, Miniard, & Engel, 2006); and

(3) degree of ubiquity. With regard to (1) cloud-based 4Ps, marketing mix variables are planned and programmed in the cloud. Marketers and advertisers attempt to motivate consumers to access the cloud through a diverse range of access points, including social networking sites. Upon completion of HTML5, the contents will be more standardized and reachable, regardless of the type of hardware. A mobile device will be merely one option but could influence consumers' decision-making process in a more time-location flexible manner, compared with other media. The extent to which mobile marketing drives consumer choice would depend primarily on the configuration of marketing mix stimuli or 4Ps—namely, product, price, promotion, and retailing. However, we propose to replace promotion with integrated marketing communications, or IMC, since the latter is more appropriate, given the fact that a single campaign seldom works effectively without being combined with other components of the marketing communication mix.

As for (2) CD process, our model uses a five-step approach that is simpler than the original seven-step model. In the first phase, customers recognize their need, then start an external information search. In the second phase, consumers are exposed to market stimuli, such as information and persuasive communication, leading to pre-purchase evaluation in the third phase. In the fourth phase, consumers choose one retailer over another and then make in-store purchase decisions. In the fifth phase, after the purchase is made, consumers take possession of the product and experience a sense of either satisfaction or dissatisfaction. We believe that consumer behavior orientation is more adequate than strategic/tactical marketing orientation, because this approach enables us to better understand what kind of stimuli consumers might need to receive from a mobile device during their purchase decision, not what firms should do with mobile devices. This is consistent with the basic definition of marketing—satisfaction of consumer needs.

Finally, (3) the degree of ubiquity or time and spatial flexibility is a unique and essential element in mobile marketing, which divides hand-held devices and PC or wireless and wired Internet. This size-based typology, however, is becoming more and more unclear since the introduction of intermediate devices such as the palm-top PC, tablet PC, and e-book, among others. Still, the portable and personal nature of the mobile device is an important resource from a marketing perspective. Newer versions of smartphones are equipped with a diverse range of applications yet allow instant or immediate access. Such immediacy allows consumers to manage several tasks simultaneously. We define all these unique elements—portability, immediacy, simultaneity, speed, and personalization—as ubiquity, which is conceptualized to vary, depending upon the type of stimuli that consumers seek from mobile marketers and advertisers.

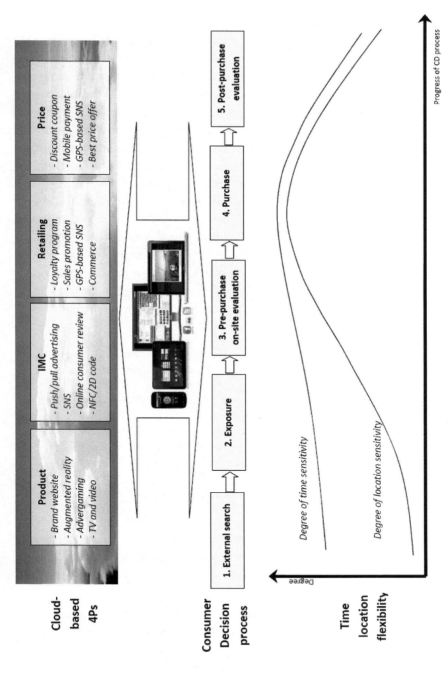

Fig. 3.2. Mobile Marketing Model. Source: Own elaboration.

External search

The search for information could be internal or external. While internal search refers to knowledge retrieval from memory, external search means information collection from peers, family, and the marketplace. External search occurs when consumers seek relevant information from their surroundings to solve a problem once it is recognized and when the resolution cannot be reached through internal search. However, external search also occurs without problem recognition, as in the case of acquiring information for possible later use. When consumers attempt to solve a particular problem that requires a timely and quick solution, the mobile device is the most suitable medium. Enhanced touch-screen quality enables consumers to easily browse the Internet with a mobile device and even check some details or specs. Although a common social belief may suggest that consumers prefer desktop or laptop PCs over mobiles due to the larger-size screen, a wide variety of apps are available for external search. When a PC is unavailable in close proximity, consumers may use these apps or browse mobile Web sites to search for information.

Based on Hoyer and MacInnis (2001), mobile-based external information sources can be classified into five major groups:

1. Retailer search. Virtual visits, voice-calls, or e-mails to stores or dealers by smartphone users, which may include the examination of package information or pamphlets about brands.
2. Media search. Information from push/pull as banners, brand Web sites, and other types of marketer-produced communications.
3. Interpersonal search. Advice from friends, relatives, neighbors, and/or other consumers who are connected to SNS, blogs, messengers, chats, or any other online communities.
4. Independent search. Contact with independent sources of information through search engines or GPS maps.
5. Experiential search. The use of product-based apps or product/service trials, or the experience of using the product online.

Some of these apps are not limited to external search and could be extended to other phases of the CD process as we will see in subsequent sections.

Exposure

Exposure is the process by which the consumer comes into physical or virtual contact with marketing stimuli. Marketing stimuli are based on information communicated by either the marketer (e.g., brand symbols, packages, signs, prices) or nonmarketing sources (e.g., media, word of mouth). The role of mobile marketing in the exposure phase has increased considerably in recent years. Advances in augmented reality (AR) have resulted in breakthroughs in the way consumers are exposed to products or brands. AR is a direct or an indirect view of a real-world environment whose elements are augmented by computer-generated sensory input such as sound, video, graphics, or GPS data. Because the crucial part of exposure is building up attention, AR could be a very useful tool to enhance consumers' attention to marketing stimuli.

McDonald's is increasing "Happy Meal" sales by using mobile marketing to engage consumers of all ages via a worldwide Smurfs (a group of small, blue, imaginary creatures) campaign that includes augmented reality and mobile check-ins. The company is running the Smurfs promotion in North America, Latin America, and Europe. The promotion is part of a new global Happy Meal program tied to a health and eco-friendly theme: it encourages kids and families to be friends of the planet and focuses on the great taste of fruits and vegetables. Mobile activations and in-restaurant avatar items will unlock additional fun with Smurfs for customers. Mobile is just one of the ways that consumers can unlock additional features, as they can also access it via the Web. For example, in the U.K., a Smurfs drawing competition invites children to receive their own mini Smurf flower garden and the chance to win a Smurfs gardening kit. Happy Meals will feature up to 10 specially designed Smurf toys that capture their unique personalities (Mobile Commerce Daily, 2011).

One of the most popular AR applications, Google Goggles, uses image recognition technology that enables consumers to snap a photograph of an object and automatically search for results based on images and text within the photo. This application is capable of recognizing brands, famous landmarks, storefronts, and artwork, among other items. For example, if you were walking down the street and saw a new car you liked, taking a snapshot of the trim level or logo could return the results. Furthermore, Google Goggles allows consumers to see location- and direction-specific Google Maps results by pointing a camera in any direction. Goggles uses data from the phone's GPS and compass to deliver live, augmented-reality results. The app places a button with the business name at the bottom of the screen. Tap the button, and Goggles loads information about the business from a Web search (PCWorld, 2009).

Virtual exposure to products or brands is a reality. Airwalk used AR to create an invisible pop-up store. To access the stores, customers downloaded the application to their smartphones and then (physically) visited Venice Beach in Los Angeles and Washington Square Park in New York City. Upon arrival, they were able to capture the virtual shoes that were linked via GPS to each location on their phone. They were then taken to the Airwalk e-commerce site and given a pass code link to complete their purchase. Mobile Marketing in Action 3.2 describes Airwalk's first mobile shop in collaboration with GoldRun.

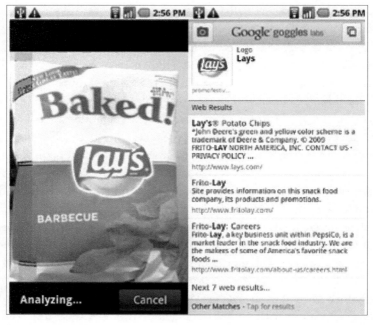

Fig. 3.3. Google Goggles.

Note: When consumers capture an image, Google Goggles breaks it down into object-based signatures. It then compares those signatures against every item it can find in its image database. Within seconds, it returns the results, ordered by rank. Source: PCWorld (2009).

Pre-purchase on-site evaluation

In the next stage of the CD process, consumers evaluate alternative options identified during the previous phases. Consumers use new or preexisting evaluations stored in memory to select products, services, brands, and shopping sites that would lead to their satisfaction with the purchase. The standards and specifications used to compare different alternatives vary according to the individual and his or her environment. Such criteria tend to reflect an individual's needs, values, lifestyles, and so forth (Blackwell et al., 2006).

Mobile devices could provide significant support for this stage, since the mobile device allows consumers to make comparisons and evaluations, irrespective of time and location. That is, evaluative criteria can be renewed or updated in a timely fashion, wherever they evaluate their choices. Pre-purchase, on-site evaluation can be carried out when shoppers are physically visiting stores and shops. Several apps are available for smartphones that enable consumers to scan bar codes or use location-based services to find out what options (e.g., price, model, format, outlet) are available for a particular product or brand in which they are interested. Table 3.2 shows some examples. Many of these apps use a product review or assessment platform, along with some social networking functions in which shoppers publish their post-purchase opinions. The reviews can be either positive or negative, but usually require user log-in or identification. Many reviewers provide a numeric rating of the product as part of the process. Such reviews can serve as a significant information source for pre-purchase evaluation. Consumers are faced with a range of information that can potentially influence search or purchase decisions (Sparks & Browning, 2011), since they then tend to make referrals to other site users.

Purchase

After deciding whether or not to purchase, consumers choose a distribution channel and then take possession of the product or brand. A mobile device could offer an alternative channel for online sales by providing compelling reasons to shop, such as location-free operation, no waiting time, coupons, promotional discounts, and ease of payment (for example, "Best Buy"). In terms of payment, mobile marketing offers several options, including premium SMS-based transactional payments, direct mobile billing, mobile Web payments, and contactless NFC. Recently, Cimbal, or DigiMo, adopted a combination of both NFC and bar code to be used for mobile payment at the point of sale. This seems very practical, since many smartphones do not yet support NFC.

Cimbal delivers a two-dimensional bar code for every transaction. Users can start a transaction with a mobile phone by scanning the QR code through the Cimbal application. QR codes can be scanned on the Internet, in stores, on other mobile devices, and even on print format such as invoices. For transactions, a Cimbal user creates a payment request on his or her phone or the Web. Cimbal's system then produces a single-use, 2-D bar code token. The payer launches Cimbal on his mobile phone, enters a PIN, and scans the 2-D bar code. Cimbal then authenticates both parties and prompts them to confirm each other's identity. The system authorizes available funds and clears the transaction in seconds. Both parties receive confirmation receipts on their device and in their Cimbal account history. No confidential information is ever sent over the unencrypted channels or stored on a user's mobile device. Additionally, the system does not require NFC readers or extra hardware embedded in mobile phones. According to Cimbal, person-to-person and person-to-merchant transactions are free for consumers. Merchants pay a small transaction fee, but it is lower than credit or debit card interchange rates, according to the company (NFC News, 2010).

TABLE **3.2.** Location-Based Apps for Pre-purchase Evaluation.

Name	Images	Description
ShopSavvy		Founded in 2008, ShopSavvy allows shoppers to scan in a bar code and immediately discover comparable deals for that item nearby or online. Its 10 million users can access Groupon daily deals through the "deals" tab of its app. This will take into account the user's location and serve only deals that are nearby. ShopSavvy boasts 50 million product scans a month and its "Deals" function takes into account a shopper's location, shopping history, and preferences when serving up most offers.
Foursquare		Foursquare is a location-based social networking Web site that helps you connect with friends via the Web or mobile applications. The main attraction to the Web site is the race of points and badges among users. You earn points and badges when you "check-in" at certain venues or locations. Besides, you can also earn "superuser" status if you frequently check in new venues or locations and enter information about them into Foursquare. As of June 2010, Foursquare had 1.3 million registered users. The service was created in 2009.
Yelp		Yelp is a location-based Web site that offers social networking and local search services for many cities in the United States. The Yelp database contains huge amounts of local information with the minutest of details and user reviews about local businesses and services. If you are a registered user, you can post your review on any local service or business in your vicinity. The social profiles of the users and their reputation are updated in accordance with their contribution to the Web site. Yelp has over 31 million visitors every month, which puts Yelp on the list of the 150 most popular U.S. Web sites. Yelp was founded in San Francisco in July 2004.

Source: Based on First Company (2011)

MOBILE MARKETING IN ACTION 3.2
The World's First Invisible Pop-Up Store

GoldRun is an augmented reality mobile platform comprised of an app that enables users to locate, interact with and take photos of GPS-linked virtual objects positioned in the real world, coupled with an adaptive and easy to use CMS. Simultaneously a powerful promotional tool and a social network tailored for the mobile environment, the app is designed to drive traffic to physical and online destinations, increase product sales, enhance brand engagement and bolster viral impact.

GoldRun users can take pictures alongside virtual objects and immediately post these photos to Facebook. By helping brands tap into this sharing impulse, the platform turns social networks into even more effective distribution channels as GoldRun users share images of themselves interacting with everything from scenes in blockbuster films, to iconic sports figures and the season's must have fashion items.

GoldRun worked closely with the Branded Content Division at Young & Rubicam to create the world's first Invisible Pop Up Store, selling limited edition Airwalk sneakers available exclusively through the GoldRun app. Airwalk, known for their ultimate hangout kicks,was looking for a way to celebrate the re-launch of their classic style, the Jim, that spoke to the roots of the brand and channeled the shoe-maker's lineage. "GoldRun is all about brand engagement, a platform that allows agencies to think up new ways to connect people with products. We ran with it, cre-ating the first ever Store," says Kerry Keenan of Y&R's Branded Content Division. "We are always looking into technologies to help us push the envelope and develop innovative brand experiences. GoldRun made it easy to conceive a new use for its core features, and implement a customized experience that dovetails with Airwalk's overall brand narrative," continues Keenan. "What better place to showcase these lim-ited-run replicas than in the parks and beaches that made Airwalk famous."

On Saturday, November 6th, people who wanted a pair of these Airwalks—the Ladies Jim Plastic and the Mens Jim Tennis—simply downloaded the GoldRun app, and headed to Venice Beach,

Los Angeles or Washington Square, New York City to capture virtual versions of the sneakers GPS-linked to each location. They were immediately given an exclusive pass code link to complete their purchase of one [of] the only 300 pairs produced by Airwalk.

The Airwalk Invisible Pop Up Stores mark the second major promotion for GoldRun within their first week of launch, with user-controlled, virtual catwalks for H&M running through Wednesday. "The Airwalk collaboration was important for several reasons," says GoldRun CEO Vivian Rosenthal. "It shows that GoldRun is not an isolated app for one brand, but a true mobile ad platform that can host many different promotional programs for all types of organizations."

Equally important, The Invisible Stores highlighted the versatility of GoldRun. "We know that working with agencies like Young & Rubicam is vital," continues Rosenthal. "Less than a week after we debuted, we see creative minds already developing a deep understanding of GoldRun's potential uses, and designing pro-grams that will help the platform to continually evolve." Opening up GoldRun to a variety of agencies and clients is part of the startup's overall plan to help brands take advantage of influential shifts in the technology and advertising sectors. "For us, GoldRun is the culmination of significant marketing industry trends: moving away from campaigns to a relationship-based paradigm, and the ascendance of the mobile interactive space," says Daniel Crowder, Chief Innovation Officer for Goldrun. "We use features totally unique to the new breed of mobile devices to cre-ate a huge amount of brand intimacy using augmented reality."

With the explosion in smartphone sales and increasing recognition of the power of mobile marketing, GoldRun's protean platform provides a flexible and respon-sive solution for organizations looking to extend brand presence and expand dis-tribution channels. "We can deliver discounts and host sweepstakes for H&M while simultaneously selling limited edition products for Airwalk," says VP of Creative

Shai Rao. "That really excites us as it shows that GoldRun can maintain the ingenuity and creative vision that define a brand, while translating their objectives and overall values into the mobile space."

Source: Dexigner (2010). Used by permission.

Post-purchase evaluation

The apps introduced in pre-purchase evaluation can serve again in this category. In particular, those apps with rating and networking functions are becoming increasingly important as information sources for shoppers. These channels of communication empower individuals with the ability to distribute information. Other examples come from the travel industry. Popular online consumer review sites, such as TripAdvisor, Foursquare, Gowalla, tripwolf, VirtualTourist, and IgoUgo, include not only comprehensive travel-specific information but also the capability of quick circulation of their feedback or opinions through electronic word of mouth (eWOM). Prior research defines eWOM as any positive or negative statement digitally disseminated and circulated by potential, actual, or former customers about a product or company (Hennig-Thurau et al., 2004). Because travel and tourism services are intangible and cannot be evaluated before consumption, the recommendations of individuals who have experienced the service become a pivotal part of the decision-making process (Litvin, Goldsmith, & Pan, 2008). With these online information sources, consumers are able to access not only opinions from close friends, family members, and co-workers, but also the views of strangers from all over the world who may have used a particular product or service (Pan, MacLaurin, & Crotts, 2007).

According to PhoCusWright (2009), nine out of ten cyber travelers read (and trust) online reviews on tourism services (hotels, restaurants, and destinations). Additional functions of these online consumer review sites are linked with the capability of geolocalization, with which tourists could seek recommendations for nearby travel spots or restaurants while they are vacationing. Consequently, from a business perspective, tourism marketers cannot ignore the role of these sites in distributing travel-related information (Xiang & Gretzel, 2010; Sparks & Browning, 2011).

Summary

This chapter proposes and explains a new framework of mobile marketing based on cloud computing. In response to the concept of cloud computing, marketing mix variables will be standardized and stored in a virtual space that consumers can access through a diverse range of devices, including smartphones. Our intention is not to adopt cloud computing as used in computer science, but to use this concept as a new frame of holistic online marketing. The development of HTML5 will enable marketers and advertisers to develop uniform contents related to product, price, IMC, and retailing, that can be downloaded from various access points. Our mobile marketing model also explicates five phases of the consumer decision process. In each phase, various types of applications can be used according to the degree of time-location flexibility.

NOTES

1. The HTML5's WebSocket JavaScript interface facilitates the message transmission between client and server and thus simplifies much of the complexity surrounding bi-directional Web communication and connection management.
2. An electromechanical device that will measure acceleration forces.
3. Scalable Vector Graphics is a text-based graphics language that describes images. SVG files are compact and provide high-quality graphics on the Web, in print, and on resource-limited hand-held devices.

4

Ubiquity

Conceptualizing Time and Space

The mobile marketing community unanimously claims that ubiquity—the usage flexibility of time and location—represents the most important feature of the mobile Internet. For example, in one of his early articles, Barnes (2002) listed other possible determinants of consumer information processing such as social norms, user motives, mode, time and location, and personal characteristics. He stressed context dependence (time and location) as the most important and distinctive asset of this advertising medium. He argued that ubiquitous interactivity would provide customers with an unprecedented level of control over what they see, read, and hear. In addition, mobile devices would enable firms to personalize content by tracking personal identity and capturing customer data: "the ultimate goal is for the user to feel understood . . . simulating a one-to-one personal relationship" (p. 413). In fact, prior research has incorporated interactivity in explanatory models of mobile marketing (e.g., Choi, Hwang, & McMillan, 2008). However, these studies provide only anecdotal evidence of interactivity, leaving a fundamental question unanswered: is ubiquity the same as interactivity? If not, how does it differ?

Unfortunately, the detailed analysis of the ubiquity concept has long been neglected, leaving it as one of the pending issues that we must explore. This chapter therefore attempts to take the first step toward the thorough conceptualization of ubiquity in mobile marketing.

Preliminary view: What is ubiquity?

The Merriam-Webster Dictionary defines "ubiquitous" as "existing or being everywhere at the same time." In computer science, the concept of *ubiquitous computing* derives from the Xerox Palo Alto Research Center (PARC), in which each user continuously interacts with new kinds of wirelessly interconnected computers. There, computers are available but invisible to the users throughout the physical environment. Weiser (1993) called this next-generation computing environment "ubiquitous computing," which is a complex integration of human factors, computer science, engineering, and social sciences. In his vision, computer hardware and software will become an effective part of our environment, performing tasks that support our broad purposes without our continual direction, thus allowing us to be largely unaware of them. It is in effect the opposite of virtual reality: where virtual reality puts people inside a computer-generated world, ubiquitous computing forces the computer to live out here in the world with people. Thus, ubiquity means being invisible or seamless so that it does not intrude on users' consciousness. More recently, *The Global Information Technology Report* (Pepper et al., 2009) stated:

> The goal may be simple but it is ambitious: Internet ubiquity offers connectivity to people wherever they are, whenever they want to access the network, with the device of their choosing. Ubiquity features safe, reliable, and continuous high-speed connectivity. Above and beyond Internet availability, ubiquity means that the Internet follows users seamlessly rather than users searching for it as they move about during the day from place to place, device to device. (p. 37)

Despite its importance, however, the concept of ubiquity has rarely been discussed in the mobile marketing literature. Among the few, a pioneering discussion in marketing was presented by Watson and colleagues (2002), who describe ubiquity as synonymous with omnipresence, meaning "not only that they are everywhere but also that they are, in a sense, 'nowhere' for they become invisible as we no longer notice them" (p. 334). In a context of e-commerce, Hoffman, Novak, and Venkatesh (2004) proposed a conceptual model of Internet indispensability in which they define ubiquity in terms of two major elements: (1) the different segments of society using the Internet and the contexts of use, and (2) the access points for its use. They claim, "the underlying idea is that as more segments of the population use the Internet in different contexts (work, family, school, etc.), the greater its diffusion and potential impact. Similarly, the greater the access points for the Internet the greater its use and impact." Thus, it is the access points that directly impact the nature of Internet users' daily routines and activities. This seems closer to a general definition of ubiquity in mobile computing, which is a generic term used to refer to a variety of devices that allow people to access data and information from wherever they are. Thus, in a way, Hoffman and fellow researchers (2004) view ubiquity as a separate concept from interactivity. In a retailing context, Kleijnen, de Ruyter, and Wetzels (2007) define ubiquity as "the ability it offers to engage in commerce anytime and anywhere." This is similar to what Okazaki, Li, and Hirose (2009) envisaged in an advertising context—the combination of time and place flexibility.

However, unlike the theoretical development of interactivity, online marketing in general and mobile marketing in particular have seldom attempted a theoretical construction of ubiquity that explains, defines, and specifies the essence of this unique concept. In doing so, this chapter seeks a multidisciplinary approach that combines perspectives from a scientific discipline called "time-geography," marketing, and communication.

Conceptualization of ubiquity

Hägerstrand's time-space perspectives

The time-space perspectives stem from the work of Torsten Hägerstrand at the University of Lund, Sweden. He focused on the organization of activities into temporal and spatial terms that can be employed to define the performance of human activities. This was the very first step in so-called *time-geography*, an attempt to stress factors associated with the spatial and temporal spread of innovations within particular environments. More precisely, Lenntorp (1999) describes time-geography as follows:

> Time-geography constitutes a foundation for a general geographical perspective. It represents a new structure of thought under development, which attempts to consolidate the spatial and temporal perspectives of different disciplines on a more solid basis than has thus far taken place. Time-geography is not a subject area per se, or a theory in its narrow sense, but rather an attempt to construct a broad structure of thought which may form a framework capable of fulfilling two tasks. The first is to receive and bring into contact knowledge from highly distinct scientific areas and from everyday praxis. The second is to reveal relations, the nature of which escapes researchers as soon as the object of research is separated from its given milieu in order to study it in isolation, experimentally or in some other way distilled. (p. 155)

Hägerstrand argues that the importance of spatial factors is demonstrated in interpersonal communications, whereby most influence is transferred within local social systems or the "neighborhood effect." According to him, it is both terrestrial and social distance barriers that impede diffusion, in that human activities form environments that have a hierarchical ordering to the extent that those who have access to power in a superior domain frequently use this to restrict the set of possible actions permitted inside subordinate domains. On this basis, Hägerstrand (1970) developed the basics of the time-geographic notation in order to have the means to keep track of both the spatial and the temporal dimensions simultaneously.

In Hägerstrand's theory, there is a "time-space" entity called "domain." A domain is defined as "a time-space entity within which things and events are under the control of a given individual or a given group" (Hägerstrand, 1970, p. 16). In a domain, activities and events are under the control and influence of specific individuals or organizations. Domains, such as a school or an office building, often serve as stations for individuals to bundle. The ability of an individual or an organization to navigate through the domain depends on three time-space constraints that characterize information technology: coupling constraints, capability constraints, and authority constraints (Hägerstrand, 1970).

Coupling constraints require the user's presence at a specific time and place, and therefore they are instrumental, physiological, and cognitive limitations. That is, individuals must join other individuals or organizations in order to form production, consumption, social, and other activity bundles. Capability constraints refer to the user's resources and ability to overcome spatial separation at a specific moment. They circumscribe the amount of effort needed for people to associate themselves with others and material artifacts at specific places and times for a certain duration in order to realize production, consumption, and transactions. Finally, authority constraints become important when several activities are intended to be packed into a limited space. Authority constraints subsume those limited-space occupations in terms of rules, laws, economic barriers, and power relations that determine who does or not have specific access to specific domains at specific times in specific spaces.

Although Hägerstrand's theory is derived from a different discipline, the concepts of coupling, capability, and authority constraints are very relevant to our conceptualization of the ubiquity concept. Telecommunication systems eliminate distance constraints for some types of activities and interactions. Over time, these systems, in addition to modes of transportation and settlement, adapt and adjust according to the development and needs of their users. The influences are far reaching, affecting economic, social, and knowledge networks. This interaction ultimately shapes users' activities and their locations in time and space. No coupling constraints—for example, presence and timing—are relevant in using Twitter or MySpace, because users are allowed to form social networks via wireless Internet connection at any time, in any place. Similarly, capability constraints become unimportant when search engines enable users to overcome spatial distance, reaching almost all spatial information at any moment. Finally, mobile banking and payment functions overcome authority constraints because the right and freedom to control specific domains at specific times will be drastically extended.

Ubiquity as extensibility

Hägerstrand's theory produced numerous successors, primarily in geography and sociology. Among them is an interesting study by Janelle (1973), who argues the importance of *personal extensibility*. The personal extensibility concept attempts to measure the ability of a person (or group) to overcome the friction of distance through transportation or communication. Fundamentally, it pertains to "the scope of sensory access and knowledge acquisition and dispersion and to people's horizons as social actors." Janelle claims that personal extensibility is "conceptually the reciprocal of time-space convergence," arguing that the rapid advances in communication and transportation technologies and their associated institutions imply a "shrinking world" with expanding opportunities for extensibility. That is, the focal point of this theory lies in the *expansion of opportunities* for human interaction, rather than the improved abilities for movement over greater distance. Of special interest to us here is the notion that personal extensibility depends on the development of communication technology, because such innovation would reduce the time required to interact with persons in distant places.

Let's contextualize the expansion of opportunities for human interaction in terms of mobile communication. Personal extensibility can fall somewhere between high and low. In a high personal extensibility situation, one can satisfy important information needs while moving away or toward a destination, by the use of a mobile device. For example, a stockbroker has just left home and is walking on a street toward a commuter train station. On the way, he turns on his mobile to check real-time Dow Jones prices, because he needs to make a buying decision that afternoon. In this case, his perceived extensibility is high, because he can access the information he needs, which he could not otherwise have without his mobile. By contrast, in a low personal extensibility situation, one stays in a static place, and thus the device takes little advantage of its portability. For example, a sales manager enjoys her quiet Sunday morning at home. She may or may not use a mobile device to check a weather forecast for her afternoon picnic, or she simply turns on her TV or laptop in the living room. In this case, her perceived extensibility is low, because she may not feel any desperate information need to catch up with her mobile.

This concept of personal extensibility and these changes in the significance of distance affect economic, political, and cultural life. For example, Adams (1995) argues that "As distant connections become easier to maintain, spatial patterns of social interaction change; work and home, resources and industries, management and labor assume varying spatial configurations" (pp. 267–268). This is precisely the result of rapid advances in the Internet in general, and mobile devices in particular.

In all likelihood, the extensibility theory can be applied not only in the mobile Internet, but also in much wider areas of portable online communication. For instance, let's think about a simple example of portable desktop virtualization. MojoPac, MokaFive, and other technologies use operating system virtualization and enable users to create a guest virtual machine that runs alongside the host computer. Typically, these technologies are not installed in PCs but can only be installed on and run from an external mass storage device, such as a flash drive (nerd stick) or USB-interfaced disk drive, including an iPod (Gibbs, 2007). Thus, you can create a greater level of extensibility that you usually carry around. This story makes us ponder the idea that mobile Internet is not confined within mobile devices anymore. The concept of portable desktop virtualization allows us to use all PC functions in a ubiquitous way. In fact, some industry specialists claim that the position of the desktop PC may decline in the long run: "Netbooks, smart phones and other constrained devices are already starting to erode the market share of laptops and PCs. As desktop virtualization enables processing and storage burdens to move away from stand-alone devices, the enterprise will encounter fewer and fewer situations where its end users absolutely need full-blown PCs" (Vance, 2009). However, such extensibility may cause consumers to feel a level of uncertainty. For example, when users access information with mobile devices on a street, they may be more cautious—intentionally or unintentionally—about their transactions. Especially when they are asked to provide personal information, they may not act immediately but save the information and get back to it later, because they may feel imprudent in doing so without giving it much thought on a street.

Ubiquity as multitasking capability

In taking it one step further from Hägerstrand's time-geography theory, Shaw and Yu (2009) claim that every point on a space-time path is associated with at least one activity, including "do nothing." They claim that mobile phones now serve as the navigation mode in virtual space to carry out a growing number of activities:

One important change introduced by the modern ICT is that we now live in a more flexible and dynamic environment of conducting activities. For example, mobile phones have freed us from the fixed locations of landline phones to stay in touch with other people. This removes the spatial constraints imposed by the landline phones. We now can purchase plane tickets on the Internet anytime in a day even when travel agency offices are closed. This eliminates the temporal constraints, as well as the spatial constraints, of visiting a travel agency office during fixed business hours and at a particular physical location. Modern ICT also provide us with additional flexibility of choosing the ways that an activity is performed. We now have more choices of conducting activities either in physical space (e.g., shopping at a local store), in virtual space (e.g., shopping on the Internet), or with a combination of both virtual and physical activities (e.g., price comparisons on the Internet followed by a physical trip to a local store). (p. 141)

Generally, our social practices prescribe the precise time and place of events, resulting in general maximum distance limits between activity sites (e.g., home and work). In this light, Janelle (2004) explains the temporal and spatial constraints that affect our everyday lives, in association with biological, social, and technological factors (Table 4.1). Technology allows consumers to extend these distance limits by reducing the amount of time required to perform a given task or to move between the places. Such advances in technology also enable multitasking capability in our everyday lives.

TABLE 4.1. Constraints on Individual Behavior

	Temporal	Spatial
Biological	Prescribes essential life-support events (eating, sleeping, and hygiene) according to distinct patterns of time.	Sets limits on the geographical range of movement.
Social	Prescribes events in time (appointments, work hours, school, holiday periods).	Allocates activities in space and the distance between them.
Technological	Frees time for other activities, allows faster response times for meeting needs, permits storage of information for use at any time.	Alters the distance that can be covered per unit of time, allows linkages between distant places, permits different levels of separation between production units.

Source: Janelle (2004, p. 88)

In this regard, Janelle (2004) further proposes four types of communication modes based on their spatial and temporal characteristics: Synchronous Presence (SP), Asynchronous Presence (AP), Synchronous Tele-presence (ST), and Asynchronous Tele-presence (AT). SP requires coincidence of individuals in both space and time. AP requires coincidence in space, but not in time. ST requires coincidence in time, but not in space. Finally, AT does not require coincidence in either space or time. The SP and AP types of interactions require physical presence in an interaction, and thus can be adequately explained by the classic time-geographic framework that focuses on the movements in physical space. By contrast, the ST and AT types of interaction are becoming more common in our modern information society, where mobile phones and the Internet have enabled us to participate in an increasing number of activities and interactions via tele-presence. According to Schwanen and Kwan (2008), the rapid penetration of mobile communications, the static spatial frameworks based on fixed locations, and the distances between those locations are no longer adequate for understanding urban travel.

Based on prior conceptualizations of communication modes (e.g., Golledge and Stimson, 1997; Janelle, 2004; Parkes and Thrift, 1980), Yu (2006) proposes three basic relationships of space-time paths between different individuals: co-location in time, co-location in space, and co-existence. Co-location in time indicates activities in different space-time paths that interact with each other within a common time window. Co-location in space presents activities in different space-time paths that occupy the same location in different time windows. Co-existence refers to the cases in which activities occur at the same location and within a common time window.

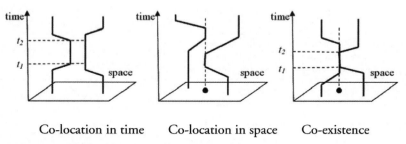

Co-location in time   Co-location in space   Co-existence

Fig. 4.1: Space-Time Path Relationships. Source: Yu (2006).

Further expanding this typology, Shaw and Yu (2009) developed a temporal dynamic segmentation model in which each space-time path is treated as a linear feature with a starting time and an ending time. This model consists of a space-time path that traces multiple physical and virtual activities in a 3-dimensional space-time system. Given the known starting time and ending time of a space-time path, any number of activities can be assigned to any points or any segments on the space-time path using a simple interpolation method. Of particular interest to our conceptualization, this model permits multiple activities or multitasking by overlapping with each other on a space-time path. Multitasking can be defined as the simultaneous conduct of two or more activities during a given time period (Kenyon, 2008). This multitasking capability seems to be a key to understanding what ubiquity enables us to perform with a mobile device.

A basic assumption underlying multitasking is that two or more activities must be spatially co-present. For example, we may want to buy a plane ticket at a travel agency while visiting a dentist for a check-up. We cannot undertake both activities because we cannot be in two locations simultaneously. However, the availability of mobile ticketing would change the situation of such co-presence, as it would "bring" the activity to us, rather than require us to physically travel to the activity. It is mobile telecommunication capability that can overcome spatial barriers to force the spatial co-presence of activities and thus enable simultaneous conduct at a single location. Through such virtual mobility, activities that traditionally require physical movement can now be performed freely, regardless of the physical location of the person undertaking the activity. Thus, virtual mobility can create accessibility opportunities. In addition, virtual mobility can overcome temporal barriers to participation, both enabling and overcoming the need for temporal co-presence. A great benefit of mobile telecommunication activities is that they can be conducted at any time (Kenyon, 2008).

For example, imagine that one day you are engaged in the following physical activities from 6 a.m. to 7 p.m.:

a. Take a metro (7:30–7:50 a.m.)
b. Have coffee (7:50–8:10 a.m.)
d. Attend a business meeting (12:00 noon–1:00 p.m.)
e. Take lunch (1:00–1:40 p.m.)
g. Read a magazine (1:20–2:00 p.m.)
i. Meet a friend at a coffee shop to talk about a trip (5:00–5:30 p.m.)
k. Take a metro (5:30–6:00 p.m.)

At the same time, a mobile device enables you to be engaged in the following virtual activities:

c. Find information about a hotel (8:00–8:05 a.m.)
f. Receive a phone call from a friend to meet at a coffee shop (1:10–1:20 p.m.)
h. Retrieve a coupon from a magazine (1:40–1:45 p.m.)
j. Make a hotel reservation (5:30–5:40 p.m.)
l. Send an SMS to a friend (5:50–5:55 p.m.)

As we can see in Figure 4.2, there are space-time paths that indicate both mono-tasking (indicated by a continuous line) and multitasking (indicated by a dotted line). This multitasking is only possible with a mobile device, because it lessens temporal and spatial constraints by increasing co-existent space-time paths.

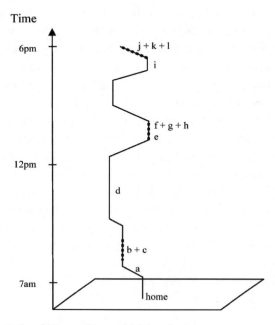

Fig. 4.2. Time-Space Paths of Monotasking and Multitasking.

According to Kenyon and Lyons (2007), multitasking is likely to be influenced by any of the following attributes:

- The degree of spatial and temporal dependence of the activity
- The necessary degree of continuity of engagement
- The required degree of active or cognitive attention

Spatial dependence corresponds to co-location in space in Figure 4.1, referring to the extent to which activities must be undertaken at particular locations. For example, taking a metro to work and making a hotel reservation at a travel agency cannot take place simultaneously. However, making an online hotel reservation with a mobile device could take place at the same time as taking a metro, because the spatial dependence of one of the activities is practically reduced to zero (i.e., making a hotel reservation). The degree of continuity of engagement in the possibility of multitasking reflects the concept of co-location in time in Figure 4.1. While doing laundry may not demand continuous use of time, it requires sporadic attention, as does preparing a meal. Because making a hotel reservation with a mobile device is only an intermittent action, it can allow us to take a break from the other activities (laundry and cooking). Thus, each is amenable to multitasking in a given time period.

Lastly, with regard to types of tasks, it has been shown that multitasking is more viable with social tasks than cognitive tasks. Social activities tend to require less active attention. Therefore, social multitasking is preferred over cognitive multitasking. In this context, cognitive multitasking refers to performing two or more cognitive tasks (e.g., doing a crossword puzzle while completing a questionnaire), while social multitasking means performance of two or more social, interactive tasks (e.g., going back and forth between carrying on a face-to-face conversation and typing an instant message) (Baron, 2008). Prior research suggests that multitasking oftentimes lessens cognitive performance. For example, watching television while simultaneously recalling sets of digits (Armstrong & Sopory, 1997) or while doing homework (Pool, Koolstra, & van der Voort, 2003) makes for poorer recall (and homework results) than when focusing on a single task. In the same vein, alternating between tasks (e.g., solving mathematics problems and classifying geometric objects) has been shown to degrade performance (Rubinstein, Meyer, & Evans, 2001). Baron (2008) claims that social activities can successfully be done in tandem, but cognitive activities cannot be done as easily because of the higher cognitive burden of such activities and poorer results when they are multitasked. Research by Pashler (2000) showed that, unless individuals are highly skilled at both tasks, the time required to complete tasks is significantly greater when performing two or more tasks at the same time than when performing them separately. One of the most widely held hypotheses underlying such a difference is that "the human cognitive system has a bottleneck for central cognitive processes that does not permit two independent cognitive operations at the same time" (Oberauer & Kliegl, 2004, p. 689).

Ubiquity as convenience

The core concept of ubiquity—flexibility of time and space—has a direct relationship with consumer convenience. People tend to use mobile Internet to seek information when they find themselves in mass transportation, on a street, or in a restaurant, because of its convenience. In this light, we may be able to develop a more precise understanding of ubiquity through the concept of convenience.

The literature on service indicates that convenience depends on several factors, including time and effort. In an early essay on the importance of convenience in consumer purchasing, Kelley (1958) cites Charles G. Mortimer's (then president of the General Foods Corporation) "ten convenience forms" appearing in the marketing system, which include time and place convenience. Time convenience is typified "by evening hours, and fresh fruits and vegetables out of season." Place convenience is defined as "life insurance in airline terminals, drive-it-yourself automobile rental services, and the planned shopping center." As time passed, the concept of convenience became increasingly important to consumers, but little research was undertaken to define exactly how it could be defined or examined. Berry, Seiders, and Grewal (2002) challenged this issue by treating service convenience in terms of consumer time and effort.

According to them, consumers perceive convenience in all products that save consumers time and effort. In service, frozen dinners are an example of a convenient good because they are easy and quick to prepare, thus saving labor. Child care is an example of a convenient service because it offers an alternative to taking care of kids while their parents need to work. Berry and others (2002) argue that much prior research focuses on goods-related convenience through retailers, leaving the domain of service convenience largely understudied. In my opinion, it is this domain in which we can develop an interesting conceptualization of ubiquity.

In light of Berry et al. (2002) and other service convenience literature, the core time-space dyad of ubiquity seems to be translated into a context of time-effort savings. First, saving time is actually synonymous with reallocation of time resource to achieve greater efficiency. Time allocation, in turn, can be seen as a consequence of demographic, socio-economic, and psychographic determinants that dictate lifestyle and consumption patterns (Holbrook & Lehmann, 1981). In addition, time expenditure has been associated with information acquisition and choice behavior (Jacoby, Szybillo, & Berning, 1976). Furthermore, time orientation has been recognized as an important cultural determinant, as people from different countries perceive time scarcity differently. In fact, a time convenience scale has been used in mobile research (Kleijnen et al., 2007) and found to be closely related to time consciousness.

While studies have been conducted on time savings, the notion of saving effort has not received as much attention in consumer research. Effort is related to the amount of energy used by consumers to complete a specific task. This can be an important component of ubiquity, because the use of mobile devices could save on energy expenditure. For example, mobile Internet could lessen consumers' effort by helping them find a specific location via GPS (see Chapter 5) or by having them scan a QR (Quick Response) code (see Chapter 6) to download coupons rather than clip them from a newspaper. In this regard, three different dimensions of effort are part of ubiquity conceptualization: physical, cognitive (the mental effort of thinking), and emotional (psychological costs).

Another issue closely related to the concept of convenience is usability. One key component of usability with regard to Web access is user interface. User interface is the environment in which online users conduct communication, information searches, and transactions. The ease of use of Web sites and Web pages is most often judged by the content, layout, and structure. These features must satisfy both sensory and functional needs in order for the user to be satisfied with the interface. In m-commerce, most limitations are attributed to the interface itself; examples are small screen size, limited screen resolution, and cumbersome input mechanisms (Cyr, Head, & Ivanov, 2006). In addition, users expect more from mobile devices, such as the ability to save time, vary locations, and personalize the interface. These factors are directly related to our ubiquity concept (Venkatesh, 2003). Mobile usability should take into account the issue of processing capacity for time- or location-critical activities. For example, iPhone's touch-screen design and user-friendly applications have made it much easier to use. In turn, it makes users feel more ubiquitous. The fact that over 400,000 different applications are sold or accessed through iPhone proves that its popularity does not come just from its screen design and manageable size, but also from the enhanced utility of the personalized content, timely feedback, and location-specific goals. In looking at the importance of these features, Venkatesh and Ramesh (2006) developed a comprehensive inventory of wireless Web site usability guidelines. Nonetheless, there is not much information available on ubiquity conceptualization of mobile device applications. Much more research is needed to expand our knowledge in this area.

Further breakdown of ubiquity

Interesting insights about ubiquity could emerge from an exhaustive review of mobile marketing or m-commerce research. To this end, an exhaustive search of the literature was attempted in a diverse range of disciplines, including marketing, management, business, engineering, information science, information management, finance, and operations research. The following databases were examined: ABI/INFORM Global, Academic Research Library, Arts & Humanities Full Text, EBSCOhost Business Source, Emerald, Elsevier SD Freedom Collection, IEEE Xplore, and Wiley InterScience. Next, we searched several keywords, such as "mobile marketing," "mobile commerce," "mobile advertising," "mobile promotion," and "mobile channel," among others. After obtaining the results, we screened out only those journals indexed in either the 2010 edition of the Social Science Citation Index (SSCI) or the Science Citation Index (SCI) of the Thomson ISI Web of Knowledge. The ISI Journal Citation Index has been recognized around the world as the most reliable as well as authoritative measure of the impact of an article on the related literature due to the rigorous selection criteria for inclusion in the index. Finally, each article was manually examined to determine whether the main focus of the study addressed mobile marketing or closely related topics, rather than programming, software, or computer technology development. As a result, we singled out only studies that offer explicit reference to ubiquity. The final result was rather surprising: only 13 articles explicitly attempted to define or conceptualize ubiquity in a context of mobile marketing. Furthermore, most of these studies view ubiquity as either a combined flexibility of time and space or time convenience. But what "ubiquity" really means still remains ambiguous.

Next, we conducted eight focus groups with general consumer smartphone users in an attempt to qualitatively examine smartphone users' motivations and behaviors. Free discussion based on open-ended questions was used. All conversations were recorded and transcribed, word by word, into text. These texts were then carefully analyzed, and important key concepts were coded. In general, these smartphone users enjoy connecting to the Internet with their mobile device because of its speed and immediacy. These attributes are inherent characteristics, because the device can be carried or used on the move. Their interest in browsing the Internet via 3G or Wi-Fi essentially lies in a motive to search information when needed or to reach a specific destination on a GPS-linked map. These consumers often use mobile Internet while they are doing something else, for instance, watching TV, listening to music, or simply killing time in a café. Since mobile devices recently gained the capability of being "always on," consumers are no longer aware if their device is on or off. This continuity is an important difference between the PC and mobile devices. Using the dimensions that emerged from the detailed analysis of the transcripts, we extracted the following eight dimensions for ubiquity: immediacy, speed, portability, mobility, reachability, searchability, simultaneity, and continuity.

Immediacy and *speed* both refer to the quickness of action or occurrence. For example, mobile portals and applications in smartphones are handy because they are accessible at the right time—when you feel the urge to use them. Immediacy implies light, effortless, easy displacement, while speed is the state of being in rapid motion. This motion fills the gap between departure and arrival, or desire and fulfillment, and refers to the manifest concrete realities of special separation (Tomlinson, 2004). Prior research suggests that instant connectivity is one of the important attributes in m-commerce, which leads to an immediate and rapid response (Barnes & Huff, 2003; Ko, Kim, & Lee, 2008). *Portability* means the quality of being light enough to be carried, which relates to the very physical characteristic of the device (Bruner & Kumar, 2005; Kleijnen et al., 2007; Barnes, 2002). Similarly, *mobility* is the quality or state of being mobile and particularly refers to something that can be operated while in transit. Gao, Rau, and Salvendy (2009) point out that ubiquity means being portable, which enables an extensive reach beyond our special and temporal constraints. Hence, *reachability* is the capability of getting in contact with or communicating with another party. *Searchability* refers to the capability of making a thorough examination. This dimension has been widely discussed in e-commerce and context awareness computing (Stafford, Stafford, & Schkade, 2004; Peters, Amato, & Hollenbeck, 2007; Pascoe, 1998). Given the increased capabilities of mobile search (which includes voice search as well as search ads), the "hit" capacity of the smartphone seems indispensable. *Simultaneity* means happening or existing or doing at the same time (Leung & Wei, 2000). As we reviewed in Chapter 1, most mobile OSs are equipped with multitasking capability, which enables users to manage multiple applications at once. This means that the use is continuous. *Continuity* refers to the state or quality of being continuous, which seems to correspond to one of the 3G characteristics, "always on." Kleijnen and colleagues (2007) see simultaneous and continuous access to services as a unique ability of the mobile device that traditional channels cannot offer.

Final thoughts

In closing, we may give some thought to the pros and cons of ubiquity. Is it always a good thing for us to be ubiquitous? Simultaneous multitasking capability is apparently a big plus for those who need to manage a busy life. At the same time, this feature—commonly introduced from Microsoft Windows—seemingly and continuously increases human stress. Speedy processing and immediate access may be a necessary prerequisite for our productive operations, and that is why faster CPU has been developed and marketed at an increasingly rapid pace. Our modern society seems now at a stage where nobody could live without this obsession with greater efficiency. Mobile Marketing in Action 4.1 provides an interesting reflection about the adoption of the ubiquitous smartphone.

MOBILE MARKETING IN ACTION 4.1

Smartphones: Our National Obsession

Doug Wilson takes his smartphone everywhere. When the 28-year-old wakes up, he snatches the phone from the nightstand to read Twitter feeds and Facebook messages before he gets out of bed. During the day, he tends to carry the iPhone 4 in his hand. Putting it in his pocket would be too risky, he said, because he might miss a photo opportunity—like that crazy "rat tail" hairdo he saw at a fast-food spot recently. ("I was like, 'I've GOT to take a picture of this!'")

And at night, access to this on-all-the-time gizmo is arguably more important than ever. First, there's the dog. Wilson uses his phone's LED camera flash to guide his steps as he takes Lucy, a bichon frise, outside. "I live in Arkansas, so I don't want to step on a snake or anything," he said.

Then there's his wife, Ashlee, whom he accidentally impregnated one evening after forgetting to look at an iPod app that explains the details of the rhythm method.

"That's how we got pregnant," he said, "because I lost my [iPod Touch]."

While the couple from Russellville, Arkansas, are now thrilled about their expected baby girl, Doug Wilson said the slip-up was yet another reminder that his phone should be turned on, in his hand, ready to accept alerts—all the time.

Otherwise, he said, things tend to go awry.

He's not alone in this hyperconnected world. It seems America is getting hooked on the smartphone. We depend on these modern Swiss Army knives for everything from planning our schedules to checking the news, finding entertainment and managing our social networks. Oh, and they also make calls—a fact that's sometimes forgotten these days as text messages become a preferred means of communication for younger generations. (Nearly 90 percent of teen cell-phone users send and receive texts, according to the Pew Internet & American Life Project; on average, they send 50 messages per day.)

Only about one in five Americans owns a smartphone, according to a recent report from Forrester Research. But for those who have purchased these devices—which typically cost more than $150—the experience can be life-changing. Gone are the days when you could wait a full day to reply to an e-mail, or respond to a text message on a several-hour delay, without violating new and rapidly evolving social norms.

Few locations today are off-limits to smartphones. That's partly because texting, internet browsing and game playing can be done quietly, and because institutions like public schools—once enemies of the phone culture—are starting to embrace these tools. Some members of the mobile generation love these changes. They say they can't live without their phones and the always-connected lifestyle they promote. Just try to watch a movie in a theater these days without seeing the glare of a smartphone screen in a nearby seat.

There are serious questions, however, about what these gadgets may be doing to our brains. Some researchers say intense multitasking degrades a person's ability to focus deeply, think creatively and, in the end, be more productive. Smartphones are among the technologies promoting this mode of thinking, where people toggle continually between streams of information.

A 2009 Stanford University research study, published in the *Proceedings of the National Academy of Sciences*, found that multitaskers—those who try to view two or more types of media simultaneously—are more easily distracted.

"They're suckers for irrelevancy," Stanford professor Clifford Nass said in a written statement about the study, which examined 262 university students. "Everything distracts them."

For these reasons, some people have developed love-hate relationships with their phones. Richard Glover, a 23-year-old political science student at Austin Community College in Austin, Texas, is dependent on his phone, he said, as much as he depends on a car to get him from place to place.

It's essential that he's able to check the latest political news all the time, he said, and to be able to respond instantly to text messages. But in 2008, he took a trip to Yosemite National Park. He couldn't get cell phone service there, so he left his phone in the hotel room.

"It felt liberating not to be connected to it," he said, "but at the same time, I was very happy to get back to it—to feel connected again."

Which smartphone is right for you?

Bud Kleppe, a 32-year-old real estate agent in St. Paul, Minnesota, said he can't be away from his BlackBerry for any amount of time. He's more likely to sell a home, he said, if he responds to client e-mails within 20 minutes and to texts instantly.

He likes that feeling of instant connectedness.

"It pretty much lives in my hand," he said of the phone. "If it's missing on me, I go into a little bit of a panic. My phone is probably never more than an arm's grab away from me."

He says he couldn't go back to his pre-smartphone existence.

"No, I couldn't see functioning," he said. "To me, it's not a curse. I love it. So I couldn't—I would probably go into the shakes if I didn't have it for a day or something."

Technology won't stop evolving, so perhaps figuring out how to manage this tech-infused, mobile life may be the way of the future. Kenny Fair, a 60-year-old graphic designer in Overland Park, Kansas, said he's had to learn to control himself and his gadgets since purchasing a Palm Pre smartphone in August 2009, an event he described as "an immediate love affair" that changed his life.

If he doesn't manage his smartphone use, he said, he can get lost in the constant "flow of information" from his phone to his head. Wilson, the smartphone user in Arkansas, said there are moments when he feels as though he disappears into the smartphone's tiny screen, particularly when he's just sitting around the house watching TV with his wife.

"I'll be on my phone looking at Twitter and Facebook and playing 'Angry Birds' and I should be showing her affection and stuff like that. Sometimes I forget to do that," he said.

"I'm just out of touch with reality sometimes because of my phone—I can just look at all the apps and stuff like that and just dream about the iPad and whatever—wishing my screen was bigger—and without realizing it, well, I haven't said anything to my wife for an hour. It's not that great."

Wilson said he's happy to take his iPhone everywhere.

At Arkansas Tech University, where he's a student, one sociology professor does not allow phones in his classroom, Wilson said. But instead of leaving his phone at home—one possible way to abide by this rule—Wilson goes through extra preparations to keep it at his side.

"When I go into that class, I put it into airplane mode and silent [mode] and I turn it off," he said.

He even uses the phone during church services.

Once, when asked to read a scripture in front of the congregation at the West Side Church of Christ, Wilson used a Bible app on his iPhone to load up the correct verses.

"I bought it for like $7," he said of the app. "It's really awesome."

Not everyone at church thought this use of technology was appropriate, he said. Several attendees approached him after the reading, he said, wondering if he was text messaging or something during his performance.

Wilson used to tote around a paper Bible. But now that book is in the trunk of his car.

Source: Sutter (2010)

Summary

This chapter attempts to conceptualize and theorize one of the most important aspects of mobile marketing: the ubiquity concept. Ubiquity is first explained in relation to a discipline called *time-geography*, then discussed in terms of personal extensibility, multitasking capability, and convenience. The personal extensibility concept pretends to measure the ability of a person (or group) to overcome the friction of distance through transportation or communication, which is especially relevant to ubiquitous capability. Furthermore, such extensibility enables us to perform multiple tasks at the same time, which is often perceived as time-effort saving or convenience. In closing, the chapter introduces preliminary results of our qualitative research that further breaks down ubiquity as a multidimensional construct consisting of immediacy, speed, portability, mobility, reachability, searchability, simultaneity, and continuity.

5

2D Codes AND Near Field Communication

Wireless connection capability is enabling brands and consumers to unite online and offline experiences. In a way, this is truly ubiquitous capability, since we no longer have to look at online and offline as separate entities: we can start focusing on the convergence of these spaces. In fact, a number of technologies are already demonstrating how we can connect our real-life experiences with our virtual world. For example, bar codes have been used as a fast, easy, accurate, and automatic product-tracking method in industrial production and retailing. But mobile phones have changed the *raison d'être* of bar codes. More generally, 1D (one-dimensional) bar codes, 2D (two-dimensional) bar codes, and color-based image codes have become popular since the introduction of camera and scanning functions in mobile devices. In general, these codes are readable with the built-in camera in mobile devices. By scanning or taking a picture, users can easily access various services.

According to 3GVision (2011), worldwide mobile 1D and 2D bar code usage grew in Q2 by 52% over Q1 in 2011, with daily scans coming from 136 different countries around the world. Growth was particularly spectacular in Australia (113.8% over Q1 in 2011), Germany (89%), the United States (80.2%), and Canada (68.8%), because many brands adopted QR codes during Q2 in 2011.

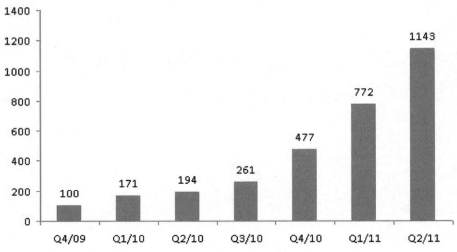

Fig. 5.1. Global Growth in Mobile Bar Code Usage Q4/2009–Q2/2011.

Note: basis: Q4/09 = 100. Source: 3GVision (2011). Reproduced with permission.

In addition, near field communication (NFC) has been receiving much attention from industry players, since Google is expected to announce a new mobile payments system based on this contactless communication technology that allows users to read information from "passive" tags or wirelessly communicate with other devices using an "active" mode. NFC support is built into two key mobile operating systems, Android 2.2 and BlackBerry OS 7.0; and, if it's added to iOS 5, it would become well established on the key consumer smartphone platforms. In this chapter, we overview these key technologies that are expected to play a central role in future mobile marketing execution.

1D bar code

The 1D bar codes are composed of serial black-and-white bar patterns representing a specific identity (i.e., encoded information) that include the Universal Product Code (UPC). The European Article Number (EAN), the Japanese Article Numbering (JAN) System, and the International Article Numbering (IAN) System are practically identical to UPC. The UPC was first proposed in 1973 by George J. Laurer as the standard bar code symbology for product marking in the grocery industry. Since then, it has been used mainly in industry and the military for distribution purposes (Kato, Tan, & Chai, 2010).

UPC has two primary components: the symbology and the coding system. The UPC symbology is made up of patterns such as center guard bars that designate the initial, final, and central positions of the image code and data patterns that encode the numeric data and the check-sum digit. These patterns are expressed in terms of the relative thickness ratio of black-and-white bars located parallel to each other. Thus, by sampling the pixels on a scan line that is placed across the patterns, the decoder can recognize the code if there is at least one scan line that covers all the patterns. After reading all the patterns, the decoder verifies the result by using the check-sum digit in the data patterns, but it cannot correct any errors. The UPC represents the number system consisting of the following:

0: Standard UPC number
1: Reserved
2: Random weight items marked at the store
3: National Drug Code and National Health Related Items code
4: In-store marking without format
5: UPC Coupon
6: Manufacturer identification number
7: Manufacturer identification number
8: Reserved
9: Reserved

Fig. 5.2. 1D Bar Code. Source: ReviseComputing.co.uk (2012).

The manufacturer code is a five-digit number specifically assigned to the manufacturer of the product. The product code is a five-digit number that the manufacturer assigns for a particular product. Every different product and every different packaging or size gets a unique product code. In addition, there are "3 guard bars" (or guard patterns) which are located at the beginning, middle, and end. The beginning and ending guard bars are encoded as a "bar-space-bar" or 101. The middle guard bar is encoded as "space-bar-space-bar-space" or 01010. The guard bars "tell" the computer scanner when the manufacturer and product code begin and end. The check digit, also called the "self-check" digit, is on the outside right of the bar code. The check digit is an "old-programmer's trick" to validate the other digits (Kato et al., 2010).

The UPC can be printed on packages using a variety of printing processes. The basic version of UPC is usually the version seen on retail store items. The format allows the symbol to be scanned with any package orientation.

QR code

Definition and features

In comparison with 1D bar codes, most 2D bar codes encode high-density data for representing a larger amount of data within a smaller size; however, 2D bar codes have more complex code structures. 2D bar codes have advanced in various aspects, including security, error detection and correction capability, and the ability to encode different languages (Kato et al., 2010). The ability to encode a robust portable data file has made 2D symbologies attractive regardless of their extra space requirements. Accordingly, industries and organizations in various fields have adopted applications that use 2D bar codes within their systems, including retailing and promotion. The most representative 2D bar codes in terms of mobile Internet service are QR code, trill code, data matrix, Microsoft Tag, and BeeTagg, among others (Figure 5.3). In this section, we discuss QR code. Microsoft Tag will be explained in the next section.

Fig. 5.3. Examples of 2D Bar Codes for Mobile Applications.
Left to right: QR code, trill code, data matrix, Microsoft Tag, and BeeTagg.

QR code is a type of two-dimensional bar code developed in 1994 by Denso Wave, which was a division of Denso Corporation at the time. QR code was originally developed for tracking parts in vehicle manufacturing and was then standardized by AIM International, JIS, and ISO (Denso Wave, 2010).

QR code consists of seven elements: a finder pattern; a timing pattern; an alignment pattern and quiet zone (forming the function patterns); and the format information, separator, and data areas (forming the encode area). Figure 5.4 shows the structure of QR code. The finder pattern is also referred to as the position detection pattern; its three blocks are located at the three corners of the QR symbol. Between these blocks are dotted lines that make up the timing pattern. The alignment pattern consists of smaller blocks throughout the code; they are in fixed positions with an isolated cell at the center of each block. Each QR code is made up of a four-module-wide quiet zone (two-module-wide for micro QR code). The function patterns, consisting of the alignment pattern and the quiet zone, define the accurate position of the symbol, the symbol size, its orientation, and the whole aspect of the symbol. The data field includes Reed-Solomon codes as well as raw data. The format information includes the symbol version, the error correction level, and the mask number.

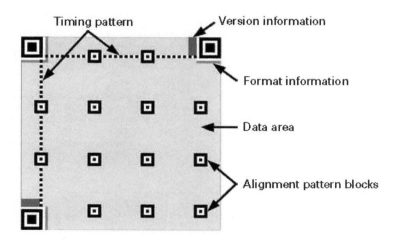

Fig. 5.4. Timing Pattern, Alignment Pattern, and Data Area in QR Code. Source: Kato et al. (2010). Reproduced with permission.

TABLE 5.1. QR Code Features

Image	Features
ABCDEFGHIJKLMNOPQRSTUVWXYZABCD EFGHIJKLMNOPQRSTUVWXYZABCDEFGH IJKLMNOPQRSTUVWXYZ012345678901 23456789012345678901234567890 123456789ABCDEFGHIJKLMNOPQRSTUV WXYZABCDEFGHIJKLMNOPQRSTUVWXYZ ABCDEFGHIJKLMNOPQRSTUVWXYZ0123 4567890123456789012345678901 4567890123456789ABCDEFGHIJKLMN OPQRSTUVWXYZABCDEFGHIJKLMNOPQR	QR code is capable of handling all types of data such as numeric (up to 7,089 characters), alphabetic (up to 4,296 characters), Kanji/Kana/Hiragana (up to 1,817 characters), binary (up to 2,953 bytes), and control codes.
1 2 3 4 5 6 7 8 9 0 1 2 5	Since QR code carries information both horizontally and vertically, we can encode the same amount of data in approximately one-tenth the space of a traditional bar code. For a smaller printout size, micro QR code is available.
ＱＲコードは漢字・ かなを効率よく表現 することができます。	As it was originally developed in Japan, QR code is capable of encoding JIS Level 1 and Level 2 Kanji character sets. In the case of Japanese, one full-width Kana or Kanji character is efficiently encoded in 13 bits, allowing QR code to hold 20% more data than other 2D symbols.
	QR code has error-correction capability. Data can be restored even if the symbol is partially dirty or damaged. A maximum of 30% of coded content can be restored.
Position detection patterns · Data area · Module	QR code is capable of 360-degree (omni-directional), high-speed reading. QR code accomplishes this task through position detection patterns located at the three corners of the symbol. These position detection patterns guarantee stable high-speed reading, circumventing the negative effects of background interference.
	QR code can be divided into multiple data areas. Conversely, information stored in multiple QR code symbols can be reconstructed as single data symbols. The data symbol can be divided into up to 16 symbols, allowing printing in a narrow area.

Source: Based on Denso Wave (2010)

QR code has been used in a wide range of applications such as manufacturing, logistics, and sales. QR code has many advantages compared to other two-dimensional bar codes. First, it has the mixed features of other bar codes such as large capacity, small printout size, and high-speed scan. Second, QR code is also open to the public; thus, anyone can use it without a license. It is easily created with free software and a conventional printer (Denso Wave, 2010). For example, there are many Web sites where users can easily encode information into QR codes and print them out. Third, a mobile phone with a camera can become a bar code reader with software. It is then easy for mobile phone users to scan QR code with their mobile cameras.

Even if a mobile device is not equipped with QR code readers, there are some add-on tools that decode QR codes simply by positioning the device in front of the code. The decoding is carried out automatically within the streaming flow, and the user doesn't have to take a picture of the QR code. Examples are QuickMark and i-nigma readers, which are free tools using this technique that are available for many manufactured models and devices. QuickMark provides extension functionalities to QR codes by allowing partial or entire encryption of codes.

As the usage rate proliferates, many engineers have refined decoding algorithms, and resolutions of mobile cameras have become higher. These improvements allow mobile users to scan QR codes more quickly and in different situations. The design of QR codes has also developed. Denso Wave introduced micro QR codes, which are smaller than traditional QR codes (Denso Wave, 2010). Further, IT DeSign developed designer QR codes, which include a picture or logo on the QR code. Because of these developments, QR codes have become more flexible and attractive. Considering these features, Li and Dou (2008) pointed out that QR codes provide less intrusive and more engaging communication tools to consumers.

QR codes could contain a diverse range of information, including Web site URLs, e-mail addresses, product images, and coupons. The primary benefit of QR code is its ease of use: by simply scanning the code with a mobile device, a consumer can be directly linked to the advertiser's brand campaign Web site. Since a QR code reader is now often preinstalled in mobile phones, it has become more and more popular in Japan. According to a recent survey, as many as 88.4% of mobile users have a QR code reader with their mobile devices, and 83.6% have actually used and accessed QR codes (Impress R&D, 2007). QR codes are placed on different media such as magazines, newspapers, posters, packages, labels, and receipts and play a pivotal role in bridging the gap between adverted media and promotional sites in cross-media strategy.

According to a recent survey in Japan, the most frequently used media for QR codes were magazines (23.6%), PC Internet (20.6%), inserts (20.0%), packages (14.4%), newspapers (8.9%), receipts (6.5%), outdoor advertising (2.7%), and business cards (2.0%). The most popular sources of information accessed were coupons (41.1%), campaign sites (39.9%), map or traffic information (11.3%), and

Fig. 5.5. A Designer QR Code.

Tokyo-based creative agency SET teamed Takashi Murakami with Louis Vuitton to create a distinctive code featuring one of the artist's characters and the classic LV pattern. Source: SET (2009).

music or video (6.1%). In terms of access frequency, there were clear differences in terms of gender and age. Females (12.2%) outweigh males (7.6%) in scanned QR code use. Younger consumers in their 20s are more active users (18.1%), followed by those in their 30s (12.5%) and 40s (10.0%) (*The Yomiuri Shimbun*, 2008).

QR codes have been used in many countries, including the United States, China, and European nations. For example, in the United States, Ralph Lauren introduced QR code in August 2008, placing it in its print advertising, store windows, and mailers during the U.S. Open tennis tournament. In this case, the user was directed immediately to a mobile site. At the site, mobile users could check out a Ralph Lauren style guide, watch videos, and read articles about the U.S. Open (Parry, 2008). If mobile users become familiar with QR codes, advertisers can integrate many communication tools within mobile phones. In 2009, Google launched "Favorite Places on Google," which includes venues in over 9,000 towns and cities across the country that will have a Google-created (and QR-enabled) sticker in their windows (Google, 2009). In the U.K., Pepsi launched its first mass campaign with QR code in 2008 by printing numbers on 400 million cans. Harrods also placed QR code in its print and online ads for a recent advertising campaign (New Media Age, 2008).

Smartphones are increasingly deployed as readers for bar codes, in particular via the three most popular App Stores: iPhone App Store, Android Market, and BlackBerry App World. The applications, such as RedLaser on iPhone and ShopSavvy on Android, allow one to scan a bar code on a product or object and get more information about it. Consumers can access product information via mobile phone by scanning QR codes. GS1 Mobile Com is working with retailers and manufacturers including Carrefour, Nestlé, L'Oréal, and Procter & Gamble to promote this technology. Mobile Marketing in Action 5.1 describes the latest news on QR code marketing in New York City.

In 2000, QR code was recognized as a national standard in China. There are now 40 versions of QR code, four levels of error correction, and maximum symbol size that can encode 7,089 numeric data or 4,296 alphanumeric data (or more than 1,000 Chinese characters). In 2007, China's leading 2D bar code technology and application provider, Inspiry, established its strategic partnership agreement with Samsung to pre-install its self-developed mobile 2D bar code software on Samsung's handsets.

Figure 5.6. QR Code in Retailing.

Note: Mobile phones with QR code readers can scan bar codes, allowing access to life-saving product information about allergens, authenticity, and nutritional content. Consumers will be able to find the latest information about product recalls, for example the items recently affected by the Irish pork contamination crisis. They will also be able to scan the contents of their baskets or redeem coupons as they shop. GS1 Mobile Com is working with retailers and manufacturers including Carrefour, Nestlé, L'Oréal, and Proctor & Gamble to promote the use of existing GS1 standards and develop new ones where necessary so that a global application can be developed. Source: Manufacturing & Logistics IT (2009).

MOBILE MARKETING IN ACTION 5.1

Picasso as a Q.R. Collage

Walk down Spring Street in Soho just across the Bowery, and hidden between fading *Village Voice* Siren Festival advertisements and cartoonish graffiti, you'll find neon-blue posters printed with a square symbol that looks a bit like a Rorschach test or maybe an Atari videogame grid.

These symbols peek out from subway advertisements for the New York Public Library, the Flying Karamazov Brothers' show at the Minetta Lane Theatre and JetBlue package deals.

On the broad side of a building at Wooster Street and Grand Street, on the same wall that once featured Banksy's signature rat wearing an "I <3 NY" t-shirt, an image of Picasso's face was comprised of hundreds of these symbols, including a giant one painted at eye-level. If you took out your phone and snapped a picture of the code with a special application, you would have been directed to a mobile site advertising the Virginia Museum of Fine Arts' new show: "Picasso: Discover the Master."

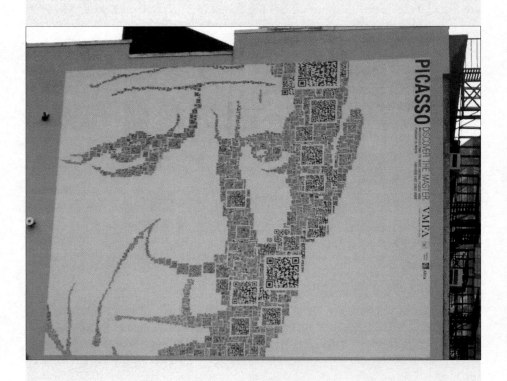

These square symbols are called Q.R. codes, otherwise known as "quick response" matrix barcodes, that can be scanned with iPhones, BlackBerries, Androids or other smartphones. Increasingly widespread yet somehow unprominent, they sneak up on you the way those long, tangled URLs at the bottom of ads used to in the early- to mid-90s. (Why would I run back to my computer to look at more of that?) But they put the man on the street much more directly in touch with the web than any URL you used to have to commit to memory. These throws have power.

The scanned code can direct browsers to a specific URL—the most popular function for marketers and small businesses who want to send customers recipes or sell them a ticket to a show. But it can also launch other actions on your phone: they can initiate a phone call, send a text message, fire off an email, open up a Google Map, or even download contact information into an address book.

Invented in Japan in 1994, Q.R. codes have been common and widely used in cities like Tokyo for nearly a decade. They are everywhere: featured on restaurant menus, mall stores, product packaging and even gravestones. A couple of years ago, in the media world, Q.R. codes were bandied about as another technology life-raft arriving to save print media by connecting the paper products to the Web. Now, with a print magazine in one hand and your phone in the other, a paper page can put you directly on the Web, the thinking went.

With the city's Bloombergification, there's been a movement to put Q.R. codes to civic use: teaching people how the city works, and giving them point-of-contact access to city data and information that doesn't require you to remember a .gov address that you'll inevitably forget to visit when you're back at your desk.

Last week, Mayor Bloomberg announced that the city would place Q.R. codes at construction sites throughout the city. Users can download an application on their phone (we recommend QR Reader for iPhone or QR Code Scanner Pro for BlackBerry). When you scan the code on a building permit, a mobile site will display details about approved work, the property's owner and job applicants, related projects, and complaints and violations associated to the location. (You might be the first to find out that the McNally's or a new La Esquina outpost is opening in your neighborhood. It's The Plywood Report!) They will also be able to click a link to initiate a phone call to 311 and file a complaint.

On Feb. 22, Bloomberg demonstrated the technology on Broad Street in Lower Manhattan, hovering a cameraphone over the code on the side of a building. The Q.R. code squared in his screen, eventually. In about 20 seconds, which seemed longer in the freezing cold, the application took a shot of the code and then displayed the construction site's mobile information on Bloomberg's phone. Success, if a bit clunky.

"Once you get this to work in one way, there's an awful lot of things you can do. And we're committed to that," Bloomberg said, standing, inside now, at 55 Broad Street, in front of a giant screen that displayed the construction information display from the phone. "The more people that download Q.R. software on their smartphones, the better this will work."

Most of his entourage, more than two dozen suits, were clicking on their phones during the press conference.

That's the upside; the downside is the same. As with all such technology, the smaller the number of people that actually adapt to the new software, the less fruitful Bloomberg's mission becomes.

And so the challenge for the city is the same as the challenge marketers and tech start-ups have been experimenting with the technology for years: getting New Yorkers to take a break from texting and emailing and websurfing on their phones to use them to interact with what's around them—see something, scan something.

Back in November we looked at Q.R. codes as one of several city-changing experiments bridging the In Real Life world with the On The Web world; since then the ecology of city-dwellers has started to catch up. Start-ups like Stickybits are handing out booklets of scannable barcodes that people can attach the city's physical grid and create Wikipedia-like mobile websites for everything from a piece of art to a corner table at their favorite restaurant.

The city has been experimenting in other, more granular ways to use Q.R. codes. They are already mounted on trash trucks and point users to a video about recycling. Staten Island Ferry riders can use a Q.R. code to watch a 26 minute [video] about city attractions and activities while they sip a post-work beer.

In June, as part of Internet Week 2010, the city's media department beamed giant Q.R. codes in Times Square for a campaign called "The City at Your Fingerprints." Displayed in rotation on the Thomson Reuters Building at 3 Times Square, the Q.R. codes directed users to websites for the city's 311 program, parks and the department of transportation. Eleven New York agencies participated in the "interactive billboard" project, with some offering a free ringtone or a chance to win tickets to a Times Square screening of the Tony Awards.

Bloomberg said his office is considering many other ways to use Q.R. codes around the city. The parks commissioner wants scannable codes so people can reserve playing times at tennis courts or ball fields. Restaurant letter grades might soon include a scannable code so diners can check out the Health Department's inspection results and find violations. Rat "remnants" found in this Mexican joint's kitchen? Let's try the Italian place down the street instead.

Landmarks will eventually feature Q.R. codes, so tourists can find historical information and other resources. They can even be useful in schools: placed outside buildings to show contact information, open hours, and historical references. Codes could be placed on classroom doors and students could use their phones to log their attendance. Teachers could include Q.R. codes on worksheets and printed packages and link students to other tutorials and extra information. Q.R. codes could be printed on tickets for school events, so parents dropping their kids off can easily queue up a Google Map directing them to the soccer field.

Q.R. codes are free to make (create your own here) and use, which is why they appeal to city agencies. They're a low-risk investment.

But as with betting on any kind of new technology, Q.R. codes may become obsolete before New Yorkers can catch on to them. Special tags already embedded in some phones can swap data, collect payments, or exchange information simply by being near another device or tag. The technology, already available in most BlackBerry and iPhone devices, allows users to simply swipe their phone near a tag, and a URL will automatically be delivered to their device or they can make a payment for a ticket—no scanning required.

The idea of paying for your subway fare by swiping your phone at the turnstile can't be far off—which seems like a more appealing use to the average New Yorker than looking up building permits at construction sites.

But at the Bloomberg press conference last week, administrators explained that the new Q.R. codes on construction sites are targeted toward the demanding, high-tech Type A-type.

"What we're doing is we're putting it in the palm of their hand as they walk down the street," buildings commissioner Robert LiMandri said at that Broad Street briefing. "They don't want to go back to their office or their home and figure it out. They want to know now."

Because if it's not now, they may not care enough to know at all.

Source: Reagan (2011). Used by permission.

In order to get a rough idea of QR code usage in Japanese mobile marketers, Okazaki, Li, and Hirose (2012) conducted an exploratory field study in Tokyo during 2009. QR codes that appeared in magazines, newspapers, posters, handouts, packages, and street signs were collected, photographed, or scanned by a mobile device for analysis. The main objective of the study was to identify (1) the type of media where the QR code appears, (2) the type of product promoted, and (3) the encoded contents. The encoded information was classified into (a) Web site URLs or (b) others, each of which was further grouped into the presence or absence of any monetary or non-monetary incentives.

Their findings suggest that print media were the most frequent type and were used in the following order: magazines, flyers and handouts, and newspapers, which together accounted for up to 80% of the total sample. Others included packages (including PET bottles, cans, etc.), receipts, balloons, and a utility pole, among others. In terms of the type of promoted product, service was the most prominent category (35%), including restaurants/fast food, real estate, education, retailing, clinics/dentists, beauty parlors, and gas stations, and others. Cosmetics and clothes were the second and third categories, representing 20% and 10%, respectively.

Interestingly, as much as 85% of the sample offered no direct incentive and was merely informational, leading to a corporate Web site, brand Web sites, or other types of publicity. Only a small portion (39 codes, or 15%) of the sample involved direct incentives by providing coupons, product sample offers, downloads, or other access codes. Furthermore, 36.9% of the scanned results were directed to Web sites, while 63.1% were directed to e-mail addresses. In both cases, these findings confirm a unique capacity of this two-dimensional code: QR code serves as a cross-media (or multi-channel) agent from print media to mobile media. Either corporate or brand Web sites were used to provide some kind of direct incentives (26%), with the former being predominant (77.5% and 84% in non-incentive and incentive, respectively). By contrast, virtually all e-mail addresses were non-incentive (91.4%), from which users were requested to send personal information for registration purposes.

A further breakdown of the QR codes linked to Web sites revealed that 28 codes (29%) required some kind of registration (i.e., required or optional) by asking for personal information. The most popular registration was to subscribe to "e-mail magazines" (e-mail newsletters) that periodically deliver beneficial information, including discount coupons, special sales, product sample offers, and so forth. More specifically, 15 required e-mail magazine registration, 8 required loyalty membership registration, and 3 asked for simple demographic data. The remaining 68 codes (71%) required no registration to access Web sites.

Figure 5.7. QR Codes Collected in the Field Study.

From left to right, QR codes in a newspaper manpower ad, McDonald's hamburger package, poster, real estate on-premises ad, and chopstick cover.

TABLE 5.2. QR Code Links by Contents, Media, and Product Type.

Classification key	QR code linked to				Total	
	Web site		E-mail address			
	Count	%	Count	%	Count	%
Media						
Newspaper	5	5.2	10	6.1	15	5.8
Magazine	26	27.1	61	37.2	87	33.5
Flyers and handouts	34	35.4	72	43.9	106	40.8
Outdoor ads	0	0.0	1	0.6	1	0.4
In-train ads	5	5.2	1	0.6	6	2.3
Direct mail	0	0.0	3	1.8	3	1.2
In-store/shop materials	1	1.0	0	0.0	1	0.4
Others	25	26.0	16	9.8	41	15.8
Total	96	100.0	164	100.0	260	100.0
Product type						
Automobile	7	7.3	1	0.6	8	3.1
Cosmetics	19	19.8	34	20.7	53	20.4
Food/Beverage	8	8.3	7	4.3	15	5.8
Medicine	3	3.1	9	5.5	12	4.6
Services	22	22.9	68	41.5	90	34.6
Electronics	5	5.2	2	1.2	7	2.7
Furniture	2	2.1	0	0.0	2	0.8
Clothes	12	12.5	14	8.5	26	10.0
Entertainment	10	10.4	8	4.9	18	6.9
Others	8	8.3	21	12.8	29	11.2
Total	96	100.0	164	100.0	260	100.0

Microsoft Tag

Like QR codes, Microsoft Tags are unique, two-dimensional codes that can be used to open URLs or multimedia files. They are based on a new technology, High Capacity Color Bar Codes (HCCBs), developed by Microsoft Research. Instead of using square pixels, Microsoft Tags use triangle shapes and colors to store data designed to be readable from any Internet-connected, camera-equipped mobile phone with the free Tag Reader application.

Microsoft claims several advantages of using Microsoft Tags over QR codes. For example, the size of Microsoft Tags can be much smaller than QR codes in that they take up less than 25% of the space of a QR code, which makes them much more practical. Unlike QR codes, Microsoft has developed an end-to-end solution that integrates the bar code with a standard set of Tag Reading software and a backend with built-in reporting and other functionality. This end-to-end approach makes it much easier for both businesses and consumers to take advantage of mobile bar coding and will allow users to continuously evolve the system with additional functionality. Microsoft Tags support color. However, these claims may or may not be valid from the perspectives of QR code developers. Below are some comments from industry experts.

John Scopes, co-founder of MSKYNET INC, says:

> I find some of the claims on the Tag to be misleading....To start, one of their major claims is that QR Codes have to be much larger than Tag. This is absolutely not true. I have seen countless examples of real QR Codes from japan that are ridiculously small...in fact too small to...(less than 1/4" wide). What really matters is the quality of the lens on the mobile camera itself and if it has a macro lens for smaller barcodes...QR Codes can be used for *both* direct and indirect encoding so on the technology side QR Codes are immediately far superior by allowing developers a choice (Tag only supports indirect). E.g. if I put a biz contact on a subway poster then I could use a direct encoding QR Code which will work without a data signal....However, if I used [an] indirect encoding method such as Tag then I would have to wait till I have a data signal before I could retrieve the contents of that Tag.

Lindsay Gray, co-owner and V.P. at AccuLink, claims:

> Here is my frustration with proprietary codes like EZCode by Scanbuy, Microsoft Tag, etc. While these applications have many benefits, I can't get around the fact that they can't be universally scanned by other QR Code readers. This fact limits the audience acceptance and hence poses an additional problem for marketers seeking painless acceptance by their target audience. No marketer wants their prospect to have a negative reaction to their campaign and that is precisely what will happen if my Neoreader app can't read a Scanbuy code or my Scanbuy app can't read a Microsoft Tag, etc. By trying to monetize and "own" the metrics these applications are polluting the waters for the rest of us trying to gain universal acceptance in our introduction of QR Codes to the marketplace. Asia did not have this

conflict and as a result the codes have been widely accepted. No wonder the US is struggling to get similar results!

Radio frequency identification (RFID)

In the 1940s, RFID technology emerged as a way of remotely identifying aircraft for military purposes. Since then, it has been widely used in civil aviation. However, recent technological development has drastically reduced the cost and the size of RFID tags and, therefore, extended their usage in various industries. NFC technology is based on RFID, which was developed for automatic identification systems. RFID systems consist of two components: the transponder and the transceiver. The transponder is also called contactless target or simply tag, which contains information and is attached to objects that are to be identified. The transceiver, which is also called the read-write device or simply reader or writer, can read the tag's information or alter it, if the tag is re-writable. The transceiver emits an electromagnetic signal that activates the tag and enables it to read from and possibly write to the tag. Usually the reader is attached to a computer onto which the data are passed. RFID readers are small enough to be integrated into mobile phones, eliminating the need for a standalone reader device. The integration of RFID technology into mobile phones began in 2005 when Nokia brought the first commercially available mobile phone equipped with a built-in RFID reader onto the market.

The RFID tag is comprised of (1) an electronic circuit that stores data, and (2) an antenna that communicates the data through radio waves. An RFID reader interrogates the tags to retrieve the information stored. When the reader broadcasts radio waves, all the tags within range will communicate. Specific software is necessary to control the reader and to collect and filter the information.

There is a broad range of RFID tags. For example, they can be either "active" or "passive." Active tags can broadcast even without an RFID reader, because they contain an onboard battery to drive the internal circuitry and to generate radio waves. By contrast, passive tags do not have their own power supply; they are powered using the energy of the radio wave transmitted by the reader. Also, tags can be "read-only" or "read/write." Read-only tags cost less than read/write tags, and the infrastructure is less expensive. However, users cannot add or modify data on the tag. Others are read/write tags that hold multiple pages of variable (changeable) data and/or fixed (unchangeable) data. RFID is set to be a part of the as-yet-unannounced iPhone 4G. Apple holds a patent for a touch-screen RFID tag reader and is said to be currently testing an RFID-enabled iPhone. Therefore, RFID could be a feature of the future iPhone model.

RFID technology has been implemented in a number of different areas and industries. One very well-known example is smart cards based on RFID technology, which have been used in the transportation industry. Hong Kong has been using this technology since 1997 when it introduced the "Octopus" system, a smart card used as an electronic form of payment in numerous venues. Today it is used by over 95% of the population of Hong Kong. Transport for London also uses a contactless smart card called the Oyster card. It can be used on most public transportation systems. Thanks to greater efficiency, it has reduced transactions at ticket offices by 1 million per week. This corresponds to a 30% improvement in the speed of passengers passing through ticket gates. Because each card is assigned a unique ID number, it is extremely difficult, if not impossible, to copy Oyster cards. Cards can also be canceled immediately if they are reported lost or stolen.

In supply chain management, large retail companies have implemented RFID tagging to eliminate out-of-stock occurrences or overstocking of products and to reduce theft or loss of goods in warehouses. For example, British retailer Marks & Spencer (M&S) employed this technology beginning in 2002, kicking off one of the largest supply chain operations involving RFID in the world. They tagged 3.5 million returnable food produce delivery trays that were filled with individual food items at the supplier, carried to shops by the distributor, emptied, and then returned. The information on the tagged trays is read at each distribution point, resulting in more efficient food delivery and fresher food in stores. RFID has also been used for animal tagging, particularly in tracking livestock. This is becoming increasingly important following bovine spongiform encephalopathy (BSE) outbreaks across the world. A mandatory RFID-based scheme was implemented in Australia in 2002, and a similar system is being set up in Europe (U.K. Parliamentary Office of Science and Technology, 2004). Mobile Marketing in Action 5.2 explains a recent example of RFID-based marketing by Coca-Cola.

MOBILE MARKETING IN ACTION 5.2

Coca-Cola Marketing Event Tracked Facebook Users Via RFID
Posted by Caitlin Fitzsimmons on August 24th, 2010 9:17 PM
Share 417 Comments (14)

For the teenagers attending the Coca-Cola Village Amusement Park in Israel, the event was probably just a bit of fun. But in the world of social networking and online marketing, the world's first real-life RFID event tied to Facebook was an event of greater significance.

The way it worked, according to Adland, is that visitors to the amusement park wore RFID bracelets. This allowed people to log into their Facebook accounts and then 'like' various attractions such as the water slides and video games. If the park photographer took their pic, they only had to flash their bracelet in order to be tagged in the photo.

Integrating the three-day event with Facebook via RFID was the brainchild of advertising agency Publicis E-dologic and it was wildly successful. The teenagers used the Facebook functionality "non stop." There were more than 35,000 updates each day even though the village only hosts 650 teenagers at a time.

E-dologic chief executive Enon Landenberg said: "We are continuously looking for ways to connect the physical world with the virtual world. The idea behind "The Like machine" is an ultimate solution. It is an innovative and pioneering method, and through it the possibility to involve your Facebook friends in events and experiences that are happening to you around the world becomes a very true reality."

It's a clever idea and seems like the perfect venue and demographic to test it out in. Someone is bound to try to replicate it soon—though next time an event like this takes place it might also involve integration with Facebook Places. It seems like a natural fit given that Facebook used RFID to test its location services at the f8 developer conference back in April.

Source: All Facebook (2010). Used by permission.

Near Field Communication

RFID technology has also led to the development of Near Field Communication (NFC), a standards-based, wireless connectivity technology that enables convenient short-range communication between electronic devices. NFC works in the frequency band of 13.56 MHz and is standardized in ISO/IEC 18092. It is compatible with ISO/IEC standards 14443 (proximity cards) and 15693 (vicinity cards), and with Sony's FeliCa contactless smart card system. Because of NFC's compatibility with existing infrastructures, there is no need for a separate NFC infrastructure.

The primary feature of NFC is its wireless communication interface, which allows users to perform contact-free transactions, access digital content, and connect electronic devices through physical touch, all in close proximity (up to approximately 10 cm). NFC devices can read out RFID transponders and imitate them. In addition, NFC devices in close range allow for peer-to-peer communication, whereas traditional RFID devices must be attached to a computer in order to serve as a read-write device. NFC technology combines two models of communication: the interaction between devices that have both active power supply and computing capabilities, and the communication between powered devices and passive tags.

The NFC standard supports varying data rates in order to ensure interoperability between existing infrastructures. The current data rates are 106 kbps, 212 kbps, and 424 kbps. NFC devices are unique in that they operate in reader/writer, peer-to-peer, or card emulation mode. Because the transmission range is so short, NFC-enabled transactions are innately secure. Also, the close physical range between the device and the reader allows the user to feel in control.

NFC is typically used for contactless transactions such as vending machine sales, parking meter payments, and transit ticketing, as well as applications in calendar synchronization, electronic business cards, cash registers, point-of-sale equipment, posters, street signs, bus stops, local points of interest (with NFC-readable tags only), and product packaging. As an illustration of this emerging NFC technology, France's three mobile operators—Orange, SFR, and Bouygues Telecom—teamed with the country's largest retail chains to form a consortium called Ergosum. Together they worked to push forward the date on which NFC-based mobile transactions would arrive in France. This was no small venture, in that the retailers included Auchan, Carrefour, Castorama, Fnac, Kinepolis, Jules, Leroy Merlin, and Groupement des Mousquétaires (which includes the supermarket chain Intermarché), as well as most of these retailers' financial service entities (including Banque Accord, Cofidis, Finaref, and Laser). By mid-2010, Carrefour had installed over 20,000 contactless-enabled point-of-sale terminals in its French retail outlets. According to company statements, by December 2009, 38% of consumers were able to make purchases under €25 by using the contactless feature, enabled by NFC, on their mobile phones.

Summary

This chapter describes 2D, or two-dimensional, coding and near field communication technologies that have been frequently used in mobile marketing. The most popular 2D code has been QR code, which was introduced by a Japanese firm,

Fig. 5.8. NFC-featured X-Men Poster.

Twentieth Century Fox Film Corp. is building consumer engagement around its *X-Men First Class* film via an NFC-enabled mobile marketing campaign in London. Source: Kats (2011a).

Denso Wave, in 1994. In QR code, a diverse range of information can be encoded, such as a URL, e-mail address, image, or text, and can be reproduced on any printable surface. Besides the technical features and characteristics of QR code, the chapter presents the results of a preliminary field study conducted in Tokyo. Microsoft Tag is a similar coding technology that could incorporate color, while radio frequency identification (RFID), which has been extended in various industries, is a way of remotely identifying objects. Near field communication (NFC) is based on RFID. NFC is an automatic identification system based on short-range wireless connectivity technology that enables simple and safe two-way interactions between electronic devices. NFC could be used for a variety of marketing areas, including mobile advertising and payment.

Mobile Advertising AND Promotion

Mobile advertising is probably the most visible part of mobile marketing. Gartner (2011) predicts mobile ad revenue will reach US$3.3 billion in 2011 and jump to US$20.6 billion by 2015, more than doubling each year. While SMS advertising continues as "king," search ads, location ads (tied in to maps and augmented reality applications), and video ads will show the fastest growth through 2015. Brand spending on mobile advertising will grow from 0.5% of the total advertising budget in 2010 to over 4% in 2015. By contrast, however, academic research in this area and the number of published studies to date are still limited. An initial attempt to review the research in 2004 proved to be unproductive, because very little had been published by then (Rodriguez-Perlado & Barwise, 2004). Only since 2007 has a significant number of papers started to appear, boosted by special issues of two journals, *Psychology and Marketing* in 2008 and the *Journal of Advertising Research* in 2009. One additional feature of the literature is that, in comparison with most research in marketing, surprisingly little of the research on mobile advertising has been done in the United States. This may be because the use of mobile devices has developed more slowly in North America than in Europe and parts of Asia.

This chapter provides an overview of mobile advertising in an attempt to achieve two goals. First, a practical classification of mobile advertising is provided so that we can systematically and consistently discuss the actuality of the mobile advertising landscape. Second, most recent statistics as well as academic research are juxtaposed so that readers can capture both sides of the same coin: practitioners' and academics' point of view.

TABLE 6.1. Mobile Advertising Revenue by Region, 2010–2015.

Regions	2010	2011	2015
North America	304.3	701.7	5,791.4
Western Europe	257.1	569.3	5,131.9
Asia/Pacific and Japan	868.8	1,628.5	6,925.0
Rest of the World	196.9	410.4	2,761.7
Total	1,627.1	3,309.9	20,610.0

Note: In millions of US$. Source: Gartner (2011).

Classification of mobile advertising

Barnes (2002) classified mobile advertising based on (1) push-versus-pull mode of access, and (2) simple-versus-rich advertising content. He defined push mobile advertising as "sending or 'pushing' advertising messages to consumers, usually via an alert or SMS text message" and pull mobile advertising as "placing advertisements on browsed wireless content, usually promoting free content." (p. 405). Especially for pull advertising, Barnes's (2002) conceptualization is unique in that, unlike other industry definitions (see MMA, 2009), he stresses the role of mobile portals or platforms with the capacity for browsing content for successful "targeting to achieve relevance, positive response and acceptance" (p. 408). For example, if users are exposed to an advertising platform that offers pull-down menus, click-through or call-through response mechanisms, and other interactive displays of advertiser messages, it is classified by Barnes as pull advertising. While this definition departs from a stricter definition of pull (i.e., communications initiated entirely by the consumer without a prior stimulus from the marketer), it has become a standard in mobile advertising research (see, e.g., Okazaki, 2004; Nasco and Bruner, 2008).

Barnes's (2002) framework has been one of the few useful typologies in mobile advertising. However, while the push-versus-pull dyad still serves as an important axis, simple-versus-rich content may have become obsolete as a classification criterion. Nine years after his publication, we need a new perspective. One of our primary questions here is how to measure the effectiveness of mobile advertising. As we have seen in previous chapters, enormous investments have been, and will be, made in mobile marketing planning and execution; thus marketing executives and ad agencies alike are compelled to defend their actions and the outcomes achieved. Thus it seems both reasonable and necessary to include the possible consumer responses to mobile advertising and, if possible, to seek a connection between these responses and their actual buying behavior.

Figure 6.1 summarizes our new mobile advertising classification grid in light of two criteria: (1) push-versus-pull mode of access, and (2) the level of consumer response. On this basis, the following sections describe the categories and prior mobile advertising research.

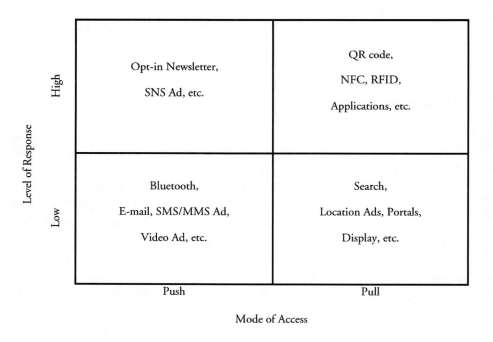

Figure 6.1. Classification of Mobile Advertising. Source: Inspired by Barnes (2002).

In this classification, there are four quadrants according to the 2 x 2 landscape. Both push and pull advertising can be grouped into high- and low-response ads. In practice, high-versus-low-response can be considered as a continuum, not a dichotomous concept. Depending upon the method and content of creative ad executions, the response rate varies. In addition, the exposure level and prior experience and knowledge of the advertised product or brand would affect such results. In general, pull mobile advertising is considered to attract greater responses, since consumers would initiate the action. By contrast, many consumers view unsolicited push mobile advertising as irritating or intrusive.

Push + Low-response category

SMS is still the most accepted channel for mobile non-voice communication. Portio Research (2011) reported that 6.9 trillion SMS messages were sent in 2010; this number is expected to exceed 8 trillion in 2011. Much earlier mobile marketing research focused on SMS advertising, including the first empirical study on mobile marketing by Barwise and Strong (2002). The authors examined young consumers' acceptance of a trial of permission-based "push" SMS message advertising in the UK. On recruitment, respondents were paid cash incentives and received more than 100 messages in the 6-week trial period. Almost all respondents were satisfied or very satisfied. The study found that 81% read all messages, 63% responded or took action, and 17% forwarded at least one message. As many as 84% of respondents were likely to recommend the service to their friends, whereas only 7% said they were likely to abandon the service. This study also provided guidelines on creative execution and tone of voice. It established mobile advertising as a research area, generating many followers, especially in Asia.

However, 10 years on, these findings may sound too optimistic, as the majority of later studies found consumer resistance to this form of mobile advertising. For example, Tsang, Ho, and Liang (2004) examined Taiwanese attitudes toward SMS advertising, using an extended model based on the TRA. The antecedents of attitude were entertainment, informativeness, irritation, and credibility, which in turn led to an intention-behavior chain. Incentives (e.g., free connection time) were hypothesized as another antecedent of intention, and permission (i.e., opt in) as a moderator of attitudes. Based on data from 380 students, they found that the respondents generally had negative attitudes toward mobile advertising because it was seen as irritating, unless they had opted in. Choi, Hwang, and McMillan (2008) partially replicated this study and found similar results.

A significant body of SMS advertising research has been published in the past (e.g., Muk, 2007; Zhang & Mao, 2008; Jayawardhena, Kuckertz, Karjaluoto, & Kautonen, 2009; Okazaki, Katsukura, & Nishiyama, 2007). These studies collectively explored consumers' attitudes, intentions, and behaviors in relation to perceived trust, social influence, and motivations, among others. However, despite the substantial number of publications, the contribution of SMS advertising research has become increasingly marginal as the gap between scholarly interests and advances in mobile information technology widens. It is rather surprising that, while mobile information technologies become more and more sophisticated, academic researchers still seem focused on the most common form of non-voice offline mobile communications. This seems to somehow crystallize a lack of interaction between industry and academia.

It has long been believed that the simplicity of SMS makes it ideal for targeted advertising campaigns that reach a broad range of consumers. However, the response rate of push advertising has been reported to be in decline due to wearout, spam, and smishing, which raise issues of privacy, security, time-wasting, and, in some cases, cost to the consumer (Okazaki, Li, & Hirose, 2009). Unless used for specific types of notifications (such as account balances or credit card transaction alerts), the SMS ads' response rate was less than 5% in 2008 (Table 6.2). Future growth (or survival) of push mobile advertising will largely depend on the industry's ability to overcome growing concerns over issues of personal data protection, virus infection, and malicious, fraudulent behaviors. Mobile Marketing in Action 6.1 contemplates the question of whether SMS is still a growing medium for advertisers and marketers.

Nonetheless, an industry survey indicates that 33% of mobile users saw SMS or MMS ads, and 33% remembered the brands being promoted (ZDNet, 2008). Furthermore, besides regular SMS advertising, application to person (A2P) SMS has become increasingly popular. This includes automated alerts from banks, offers from retailers, and m-tickets. Juniper Research (2011) suggests that by 2016 application-to-person messaging (A2P) will overtake person-to-person messaging (texting) and be worth more than US$70 billion. A2P SMS advertising, along with any cross-media SMSs, may still be a powerful tool for branding, especially in terms of recall and awareness building.

For example, SMS ads can be effectively combined in a cross-media campaign. Davis and Sajtos (2008) examined so-called LOOP campaigns in which viewers in New Zealand (Shows A and B) and the United States (Show C) were encouraged to respond to TV programs using SMS. Shows A and B were youth-oriented, magazine-type travel shows, while Show C consisted of Seattle Mariners baseball games. In each case, a "TXT and WIN" promotion was implemented: the presenters asked a question at the end of each episode or game, and viewers sent their responses (a four-digit code) using SMS. The results indicated that, due to the ease and immediacy of the mobile response channel, the LOOP communication process effectively stimulated the audience. Further, the authors argue that consumers' level of involvement, mood, and brand-related attitudes, as well as their perceptions of the cost of sending SMS messages, determined their willingness to engage. For example, viewers of a baseball game may be more emotionally involved than viewers of a travel show, thus forming more positive attitudes to the brand sponsoring the show, and leading to higher interactivity. However, if the perceived cost of sending texts is too high, the hedonic value gained from such interaction may be reduced, and the LOOP may not work.

With regard to Bluetooth-based mobile advertising, our knowledge is quite limited. Among a few empirical studies, Leek and Christodoulides (2009) examined young consumers' acceptance of advertising delivered by Bluetooth with a sample of 210 respondents aged between 18 and 29 years. They found that as many as 60% said they would opt in to Bluetooth-enabled advertising if sales promotions were offered, but only 9% would be willing to receive such messages daily. These findings imply that many consumers may perceive Bluetooth advertising to be intrusive. Still, some consumer brands have successfully introduced this form of mobile advertising.

TABLE 6.2. Response Rate of SMS Ads

Received SMS ads (in thousands)				% responded to SMS ads		
	2007	2008	% Δ	2007	2008	Δ
Downloads for mobile phone	40,792	35,915	-12.0%	4.4%	3.9%	-0.6
News or information	25,929	22,122	-14.7%	2.8%	3.2%	0.4
Mobile phone or plan	32,222	31,574	-2.0%	4.6%	4.7%	0.1
Entertainment	12,644	11,230	-11.2%	4.3%	5.1%	0.7
Total Mobile + Media Sectors	**111,587**	**100,841**	**-9.6%**	**4.1%**	**4.1%**	**0.0**
Clothing/Fashion	3,982	5,503	38.2%	5.8%	6.4%	0.6
Restaurants	1,037	1,424	37.3%	11.6%	15.5%	3.9
Cars	4,407	3,731	-15.4%	11.2%	7.9%	-3.3
Food	1,413	2,162	53.0%	9.2%	12.6%	3.4
Financial services	8,963	9,956	11.1%	3.7%	4.7%	1.0
Consumer electronics	3,957	4,647	17.4%	6.3%	6.7%	0.4
Travel	5,779	6,602	14.2%	4.9%	5.8%	0.9
Total Non-Mobile or Media Sectors	**29,539**	**34,024**	**15.2%**	**6.2%**	**6.8%**	**0.5**

Note: SMS Advertising Audience and Response Rates. Three-month average ending August 2007 and August 2008. Mobile Subscribers in EU5 (UK, France, Germany, Italy, and Spain). Source: comScore (2008)

TABLE 6.3. Response Rate of SMS Ads by Country

	Germany		Spain		France		Italy		UK	
Activity	%		%		%		%		%	
Watched video	3.7	3.6	7.9	1.5	5.5	6.9	7.4	6.9	5.2	4.4
Listened to music	19.3	0.4	24.1	1.4	16.2	2.2	16.8	2.0	22.2	1.5
Accessed news/info via browser	6.6	0.6	9.3	7.7	10.8	9.4	9.3	12.1	16.7	2.4
Received SMS ads	29.2	-2.3	73.6	-0.7	62.8	0.2	54.3	-2.1	38.2	-1.4
Played downloaded game	7.9	1.4	11.3	-4.7	4.2	4.5	8.5	3.0	10.5	1.5
Accessed downloaded application	2.9	-0.9	3.4	2.8	2.1	22.1	5.1	1.4	4.0	6.4
Sent/received photos or videos	22.1	1.0	33.2	2.0	25.4	7.7	32.8	4.0	31.8	1.2
Purchased ringtones	2.9	-6.6	4.1	-1.9	3.2	3.7	3.3	-7.5	3.1	-1.1
Used e-mail	7.3	-1.4	10.5	2.8	7.1	8.1	11.9	3.5	9.6	1.9
Accessed social networking sites	1.9	-1.8	3.5	20.8	2.5	10.4	3.0	17.6	7.3	10.0

Note: SMS Advertising Audience and Response Rates. Three-month average ending August 2007 and August 2008. Mobile Subscribers in EU5 (UK, France, Germany, Italy, and Spain)

Source: comScore (2008)

MOBILE MARKETING IN ACTION 6.1

SMS: The Dying Cash Cow for Wireless Carriers?

Over 6.1 trillion text messages were sent last year worldwide, according to a report from the International Telecommunications Union. This number has climbed steadily since the advent of text messaging, but some analysts and industry insiders predict that carrier revenues associated with SMS are going to decrease dramatically in the next few years.

Why would a once booming source of revenue suddenly decline? Two factors are pulling at the market for SMS. First, the way carriers charge for SMS has simply made the 10-cents-per-text model less reasonable for consumers. Users are texting more and are thus buying text messaging plans that bundle hundreds or thousands of text messages per month for relatively per-message inexpensive prices. Second, the rise of smartphones has paved the way for Internet-based communications that don't rely on wireless carriers' SMS channels. Apps like Facebook, Twitter, Research In Motion's BlackBerry Messenger, Apple's forthcoming iMessage and WhatsApp allow users to send unlimited messages to recipients on the same service, all via their smartphone data plan.

"We do see more people texting, it's just we don't know if people will do that with the regular text, SMS, or with the IP, with a push-based notification," said Julie Ask, an analyst with Forrester Research who is currently researching how push-based notifications will affect SMS, from a business perspective.

John White of Portio Research doesn't believe carriers will take much of a hit due to slowing SMS revenues. He said the growth of carriers' data revenues should offset the slowdown in text revenues.

"[SMS] revenues are slowing predominantly due to the long term price-erosion effect of all-you-can-eat bundles, ever increasing competitive pressure between MNOs, and new services taking market share (slowly) from SMS," White said.

Indeed, AT&T Mobility announced it will discontinue a number of its text messaging plans, including its $10 per month plan for 1,000 text messages, and will instead only offer a $20 unlimited messaging plan per month for a single line or a $30 unlimited messaging plan per month for families. The carrier's only other option will be per-message billing at 20 cents for each text message and 30 cents for each picture/video message.

As carriers phase out unlimited data plans, users will either invest more money in buying larger data plans or use their data more carefully, opting to use other messaging options than traditional SMS. Either way, the carriers should not see a revenue loss, White said.

Forrester Research's Ask doesn't see SMS drastically decreasing in the near future either. Texting and chatting apps like Facebook often require both users to have the same messaging system, she pointed out, while text messaging works across virtually every mobile phone in the world.

Chetan Sharma, from Chetan Sharma Consulting, said in a new report that the United States unseated Philippines as the king of text messaging with almost 664 messages per subscriber per month, compared with the Philippines which is seeing a sharp decline in per user messaging due to IP messaging. He said some of the European operators are also experiencing the pain of declining SMS usage. However, Charma noted that while the percentage share of the data revenues is declining for messaging, revenue growth is staying strong with almost $5 billion in revenues in the United States in the second quarter.

Source: Raman (2011)

Push + High-response category

Subscription-based e-mail newsletters are a popular marketing tool, as they are perceived as less intrusive because of previous consent given to the advertisers. Technically, users have already opted in—and can always opt out—while the information can be retrieved or accessed when they are interested in it. On the other hand, due to increasing fraudulent behavior by unethical marketers (e.g., "smishing," that is, SMS phishing), mobile users are increasingly concerned about their information privacy and security. (We will discuss this issue in detail in Chapter 7.) Industry statistics are consistent with these arguments. For example, MMA and Lightspeed Research (2010) conducted surveys in the U.K., France, and Germany, and found that the most effective form of mobile advertising was opt-in SMS in the U.K. (40% said they were more likely to respond to these) and in France (21%), while in Germany it was mobile Web ads (27%).

A key to understanding the acceptance of mobile newsletters is relevancy. Mobile users want to receive relevant, organized content, rather than sporadic, eye-catching information. This relevancy would lead to eventual action or experience (i.e., click-through). In general, a newsletter format has the following advantages over other alternatives:

- Due to a voluntary subscription, it can more easily communicate with organized content.
- It can be custom designed to reflect subscribers' needs and profiles.
- Content management and organization can be more flexible and could incorporate embedded images, videos, links, and so forth.
- It can encourage subscribers to interact with the emitter with polls, article ratings, and reader feedback.
- It can incorporate sponsor ads and promotional materials that eventually generate additional revenue.
- It can track and manage marketing efforts with detailed metrics for article click-through, social media integration opportunities, and recipient comments.

Although exact statistics are hardly available, the response rate from items published in mobile newsletters could be substantially greater than SMS ads. For example, Cross-marketing (2010) reported that more than 13% of mobile newsletter subscribers use coupons for fast food restaurants in Japan. According to iShare (2009), as many as 26.2% of Japanese fast food diners register for a free coupon service, in particular females (28.2%) and young adults in their 30s (28.4%).

As Facebook penetration reaches almost half the population of North America, SNS-based ads are increasingly and understandably popular. According to eMarketer (2011), SNS ad spending was predicted to reach $3.08 billion in the United States in 2011, with a growth rate of 55% from $1.99 billion in 2010. This dramatic growth in spending would bring SNS ad dollars to 10.8% of the total online ad spending in the United States. Worldwide, where SNS ad spending was expected to rise 71.6% to $5.97 billion in the same period, that proportion would be somewhat lower, at 8.7%. An important portion of SNS ad spending is expected from mobile media due to an acceleration in use. For example, in December 2010, 57.3% of smartphone users in the United States (36.2 million users) accessed

SNSs or blogs at least once during the month, an increase of 11.2% from the previous year (comScore, 2011). It seems reasonable to assume from these figures that SNS smartphone ads may be substantial in terms of spending. SNS will be discussed in detail in the next chapter.

Pull + Low-response category

In pull mobile advertising, communications are initiated by the consumer as in searches, mobile portals, and display ads. Among them, search ads are expected to play a central role in terms of ad revenue. For example, a BIA/Kelsey (2011) survey indicates that search ads account for approximately US$307 million, while display and SMS ads cost US$325 and US$554 million, respectively. By 2016, search ads are expected to triple to US$954 million, exceeding display (US$468) and SMS ads (US$714). The main reason for this spectacular growth is the rapid sophistication of the smartphone environment that allows users quick and efficient Web access. Because search is the front door to browser-based experiences, this bodes well for search volume, and thus revenues. Time-space flexibility—in particular, portability, continuity (or always-on capability), and immediacy—drives search ad click-through and cost-per-click greater than desktop equivalents. In addition, given the competitive push of Google's mobile business, its core search business compels it to push for a world in which the browser is the front door (Search Engine Watch, 2011).

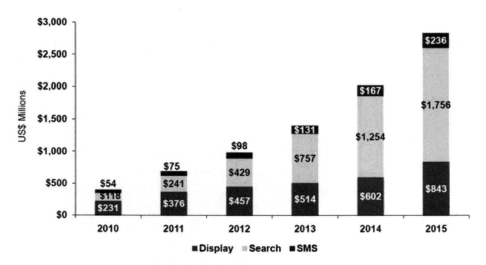

Fig. 6.2. Share of Mobile Ad Spent by Format. Source: BIA/Kelsey (2011). Reproduced with permission.

Search ads could broadly include location-based ads that are tied into GPS maps and other related applications. This topic will be discussed in detail in Chapter 7.

As for a mobile portal, much less attention has been paid in both industry and academia. This is probably because the concept of a mobile portal was not widely accepted until a touch-screen technology was introduced. When the penetration of smartphone intensifies, many corporate Web portals will be redesigned for mobile devices. For example, after struggling to reinvent itself in the image of Google, AOL redesigned its new mobile portal with Android applications. The portal provides a touch-driven interface with HTML5 support that works on any mobile browser, including iPhone and Android devices. Contents on the portal include location-based services for local weather, movies, and traffic.

This type of mobile portal was initially offered in NTT DoCoMo's i-mode service that was popular in the early 2000s in Japan. Okazaki (2004) examined factors influencing consumers' motives to click text banner ads in an i-mode portal platform called "Tokusuru Menu" ("beneficial menu" in Japanese). This platform attracted more than 1 million subscribers to freely access the promotional information delivered by various companies. The study found that three constructs—content credibility, infotainment, and irritation—affected the formation of attitudes toward wireless ads, which in turn determined the level of intention to click the ads. Interestingly, the demographic analysis revealed that the unmarried working youth segment has a higher propensity to access such pull mobile ads. The study finds that there may be an important segment that consists of single employed females who may be termed "parasite singles." Okazaki (2006) furthered the analysis by clustering consumer segments that are likely to access the mobile portal platform based on uses and gratifications theory and demographic variables.

Some popular mobile portals offer free games provided by sponsor brands for the registered users. This is a unique form of advertising called advergaming (i.e., a mixture of advertising and gaming), which can be defined as "the use of interactive gaming technology to deliver embedded advertising messages to consumers" (Chen and Ringel, 2001). Advergame types range from simply featuring the brand in the gaming environment to creating more elaborate virtual experiences with the brand. In any case, product placement is paramount, and the games are regarded as a mechanism for attracting and retaining consumers. In this way there is a positive association established between game play and the sponsor's brand. In general, games are less obtrusive than other Web forms, because consumers play games for fun, social escape, social interaction, and relaxation. Mobile Marketing in Action 6.2 provides details of a campaign by Unilever's Rexona.

Pull + High-response category

This category includes QR code, NFC, RFID, and other smartphone applications (regular applications and A2P) that enable users to access the information only proactively. That is, the information is shown in such a way that an invitation symbol is provided, but users must take the initiative. In a sense, these modes of advertising are not only practical but also experiential (i.e., proactive conduct) in that users can feel what they are getting "at will."

Since Google is phasing out QR code from the Google Places Dashboard in favor of NFC (International Business Times, 2011), some industry experts argue the superiority of NFC over QR codes. For example, Business Insider (2011) reports that

> QR code is on its way out. It's going to be replaced by near-field communication (NFC) chips that ship with phones and provide a much easier way to accomplish many of the same tasks. Instead of pointing your phone at some weird looking image, scanning it, and waiting, you'll simply be able to hold your phone up near a sign with an NFC chip and get exactly the same results.

This seems fairly shortsighted, as the purposes of the two technologies are very different. In a way, QR code is an *information-oriented* technology, while NFC is a *transaction-oriented* technology. QR code is just a bridge between offline and online information. By contrast, NFC can be most effectively used as an alternative technology of mobile payment, as NFC allows for a transaction between two devices (a phone and an NFC chip) within close proximity. This is the major difference. Therefore, when marketers have no need to engage any transactional motives, QR code is more practical, less expensive, and less intrusive.

NFC is undoubtedly a promising technology, but it cannot be printed by an ink jet printer; neither can it be posted on a billboard, broadcast on TV, or displayed on a Web site. Thus, QR codes are much less expensive to distribute than NFC or RFID. In addition, marketers can easily track how many times the QR codes have been scanned and how many of those consumers subsequently visited the target Web site. This is a breakthrough in technology when compared to the days when marketers had to print a URL on "cross-media" ads.

Fig. 6.3. JetBlue's QR Code Poster.

JetBlue created a cute ad campaign around 2D bar codes in the NYC Subway. Source: 2D Barcode Strategy (2011).

Fig. 6.4. Sony Music's QR Code Ad.

Sony Music has launched a QR code advertising campaign to promote new music from 11 popular artists on the Columbia record label. The ads appear on the tip seats inside 100 black taxicabs in London. The ads feature a QR code that passengers can scan to enter a competition to win a Columbia label tote bag. In addition, the ads instruct passengers to request the new music they want to hear from their taxi driver. Source: 2D Code (2011a).

Fig. 6.5. QR Code in Hallmark Greeting Card.

Hallmark's new line of Halloween cards for kids includes QR codes on the back leading to video scenes from Disney movies, Scooby-Doo programs, and scenes from the Marvel Super Hero Squad. This card shows a QR code for the Disney film *Cars*. Source: 2D Code (2011b).

MOBILE MARKETING IN ACTION 6.2
Unilever's Rexona runs "Detective Stripes" Mobile Ad Campaign

The "Detective Stripes" Campaign Landing Page.

Unilever Brazil is running a mobile ad campaign to enrich the marketing mix of its Rexona Invisible brand. Created by ad agency CUBOCC, the ad campaign is running on the Hands mobile ad network, which includes mobile sites such as Rolling Stone Brazil, Reuters and Nintendo World, as well as many other newspapers, magazines, sites and blogs. By clicking on the banners, consumers can download exclusive content from Unilever's international "Detective Stripes" campaign according to their device model.

"Big advertisers like Unilever require excellence in execution to reach their audience," said Edison Maluf, sales director for Hands, São Paulo, Brazil. "Our mission is offer the best opportunities to deliver the best results. Hands has many different channels and different audiences," he said. "Our network can reach many profiles such as executives, women, geeks and many others. It's a matter of choosing the appropriate publisher for each target."

A banner ad for Unilever's "Detective Stripes" Campaign on *Rolling Stone*'s Portuguese-Language Mobile Site

Unilever is a British-Dutch multinational corporation that owns many of the world's consumer product brands in food and beverages, cleaning agents and personal care products. Hands, a 10-year-old company specialized in mobile marketing and advertising, is focused on the mobile Internet in the Brazilian market.

Hands' mobile ad network has around 300 publishers. These include Brazilian newspapers and magazines such as *O Globo*, *Estadão*, *Valor Econômico* and *Rolling Stone* in Portuguese. Hands also features segmented channels such as business (AdNews, Resseler Web), sports (Futebol Total, Webventure, Webrun), local services (Climatempo, Maplink), technology (IDGNow!, IT Web, PC Magazine, Webinsider), style (Netmovies, RollingStone) and others.

The target demographic of Unilever's "Detective Stripes" mobile campaign is men 18–34 years old. Consumers can interact with video and download wallpapers related to the Rexona Detective Stripes campaign.

Hands' platform automatically recognizes each consumer's mobile phone type and adjusts the banners and sites to it. The campaign is available for more than 2,000 different devices, including Apple's iPhone and Nokia handsets.

The content available for Unilever's mobile campaign is comprised of wallpapers, video and the "Detective Stripes" game. According to the features available on each consumer's mobile device, the user can access one or more of these options. The advergame is available on Java-enabled handsets. The best players win Rexona prizes.

"When we were implementing the action in Brazil, we decided to create a mobile advergame to propose and enhance a new kind of audience engagement," said Domingos Secco Junior, digital channels manager for CUBOCC, São Paulo, Brazil. "The prizes weren't supposed to be something relevant or expensive. We've preferred to deliver products kits for the best players, because the idea of mobile games is to deliver rich, fun content that can be accessed at any time by the consumers," he said.

The "Detective Stripes" campaign to promote Unilever's Rexona brand has a regional focus on Latin America.

Besides actions on mobile portals, Unilever invested in an online campaign, which included a daily YouTube homepage insertion with an exclusive video about the game.

"Hands was a very obvious choice, because it is one of the main mobile media players in the country," Mr. Secco said. "We've reached our target—males 18–34—very efficiently in the young and technology channels.

CUBOCC is the digital media agency for Unilever's Rexona, Axe, Closeup, Clear, Kibon, Knorr and Becel brands in Brazil and is planning a mobile strategy for all of them.

"Unilever, as one of the biggest advertisers worldwide, is always searching for innovative actions," Mr. Secco said. "Right now, mobile advertising is one of those media opportunities that can't be out of the marketing mix."

Source: Butcher (2009). Used by permission.

Future directions

A decade ago, when mobile advertising research was initiated, only a limited number of countries had 3G availability, which did not enable marketers to explore the full potential of mobile media as a marketing communication tool. However, since the proliferation of touch-screen smartphones, industry has quickly caught up with the latest applications. While message-based advertising may still be the most economic and practical way to promote products and services, its revenue is expected to slow, while display or search advertising will grow substantially. From an academic point of view, there is a clear deficiency in research on pull mobile advertising, since the great majority of published research focuses on SMS advertising.

As we have discussed in this chapter, mobile advertising is finally growing in importance, especially in relation to new technologies such as QR code, NFC, RFID, and WLAN. Also, search ads, location ads, mobile portals, and A2P ads may become a growing business reality, while opt-in newsletters are gaining consumers' trust. Academic researchers should try to explore these new areas.

We see cross-media or multichannel communication as an especially promising area for future business as well as research, with the mobile channel—in conjunction with QR code, NFC, or RFID—as a fast, easy, ubiquitous response format for other marketing media and promotions. Among these alternatives, QR code can be increasingly used as an inexpensive way to connect offline to online, while NFC will be used more in relation to mobile payment.

After all, mobile advertising should be increasingly considered from the perspective of holistic marketing—in particular, integrated marketing communications—not as an independent marketing tool. Mobile advertising, specifically A2P, QR code, and NFC ads, will be more and more integrated as a cross-media or multichannel marketing strategy. As we discussed in Chapter 2, such strategy will be part of our big picture: cloud-based online marketing. An increasing number of consumers will access the information with a wide range of devices.

Summary

This chapter proposes a new classification of mobile advertising research, framed by push/pull dyad x the level of consumer response. It is a matrix based on Barnes's (2002) mobile advertising classification of push/pull x simple/rich content. Our expectation is that companies will use a greater variety of communication tools that capture a higher level of consumer response. Marketers have started to broaden the agenda to cover mobile advertising beyond SMS and mobile as a "pull" or response medium, for example, in combination with search, location-based services, SNS, QR code, and NFC, among others.

7

Location-based Services

Applications based on the Global Positioning System, or GPS, are becoming increasingly popular among smartphone users. GPS is a technology that employs satellites to give users their exact position on the Earth. For example, Google Maps can show you where you are on a street map and direct you to a desired location. Foursquare, a popular application, automatically detects your favorite restaurants in the city where you are located via GPS, and notifies your friends via social media. All these amenities are available thanks to location-based services (LBSs). LBSs are geographically oriented data and information services provided to users across mobile telecommunication networks. LBSs aim to provide specific, targeted geospatial information about users' surrounding environment, their proximity to other entities in space (such as people and places), and/or distant entities (for instance, future destinations). GPS can be incorporated into the Geographical Information System (GIS), which is an integrated network of computer software designed to capture, store, manipulate, analyze, manage, and present all types of geographically referenced data.

A theoretical explanation underlying LBS is partially provided by Miller (2005), who proposed a people-based perspective of GIS for transportation and urban analysis. In his seminal essay "What About People in Geographic Information Science?," he argues that the earlier place-based perspective was developed in an era when data were scarce, computational platforms weak, and questions simpler, and it ignores the basic spatio-temporal conditions of human existence and organization. However, such a view is no longer tenable, because drastic changes in transportation and telecommunication systems have altered the nature of space and time. According to Miller, the world is "shrinking," because transportation and communication costs dropped drastically over the last two centuries. The world is "shriveling," because relative differences in transportation and telecommunication costs are increasing at most geographic scales. The world is also "fragmenting," because people and activities are becoming disconnected from location. A people-based GIS is more suitable for answering questions of access, exclusion, and evolution in a shrinking but shriveling and fragmenting world. This people-oriented perspective on GIS approaches the rise of GPS-based LBSs through wireless communication networks. He argues that LBS technology provides specific, targeted information to individuals based on their geographic location, thus serving as an ideal vehicle for collecting GIS data.

This chapter focuses on a wide range of LBS applications in marketing. We first provide a brief overview of technical perspectives of LBS and then describe various uses in tourism and health monitoring.

Tourism marketing

Place marketing

On August 20, 2010, Facebook introduced a new iPhone service called Facebook Places that allows users to share their location with others. It enables us to *tag* ourselves at specific locations in the way that we tag ourselves in photos uploaded to the social networking site. A term used to describe sharing our current location is "check in." We just tap on the "Places" button on our mobile and then press "Check In." Everyone who is checked in to the same location can see who else is listed as "Here Now" for a few hours after they check in. According to Forrester, until now most users of location-based check-in services have been a niche group of technology journalists and early adopters, and no more than 1% of U.S. adults share their locations through geolocation services more than once a week. However, with more than 500 million active users across the globe, Facebook will change this situation rapidly (The Independent, 2010).

This is one of the typical location-based services that have been receiving increased attention in many business areas. Location-based services (LBSs) can be defined by this research as "wireless services which use the location of a handheld device to deliver applications exploiting pertinent geospatial information about a user's surrounding environment, their proximity to other entities in space (such as people and places), and/or distant entities (for instance, future destinations)" (Urquhart et al., 2004). More broadly, it "aims to provide specific, targeted information to users based on each specific user's location at any time." LBSs combine two widespread cartographic media, the paper map and the desktop Web, taking advantage of the benefits of both for the dissemination of geospatial information (Jiang and Yao, 2006).

Technically, positioning services tend to rely on one of three types of technology: (1) satellite navigation systems, (2) mobile networks, and (3) local positioning systems. First, satellite navigation systems such as GPS, or the global navigation satellite system (GLONASS), can track an object. Both systems determine the position of a receiver based on the time needed to transmit signals between the satellite(s) and the receiver. GPS was developed originally for the U.S. Department of Defense (Karim, 2004). The GPS tracking device is now widely found in mobile devices used by various industries to locate an object in an emergency. For example, in many countries GPS and Web-based GISs are used to monitor diagnostic data from hospitals in order to control chronic diseases (Ptochos et al., 2004). Second, the positioning methods developed within mobile networks rely on triangulation from various land-based cell phone towers. In the United States, these methods have been well developed due to a directive by the Federal Communications Commission that emergency personnel must be able to physically locate cell phones (called E-911). Thus, all cell phones sold in the United States now have a geographic positioning function (Chen et al., 2004). Finally, local positioning systems are particularly useful for interior locations. Such systems use Bluetooth, radio frequency identification (RFID), or wireless local area networks (WLANs) as the basic technology for the positioning function. Bluetooth is an open standard for short-range radio frequency (RF) communication in which small radio transmitters are positioned at strategic points in the environment. When one approaches such a transmitter carrying an appropriate receiver, pre-recorded information that can include anything from advertising to the identification of, for example, a bus stop, is read out. Bluetooth transmitters need an energy supply such as an integral battery. RFID is based on a passive or active radio circuit that transmits information when approached by a special combination of transmitter and receiver. As the fixed transmitter is normally passive, it does not need to have its own energy supply. For example, RFID has been used by government agencies to track livestock movements in the United States so that contagious diseases among cattle might be reduced (Gogan, Williams, & Fedorowicz, 2007). RFID is explained in detail in Chapter 5. As an example of WLAN positioning technology, tourists in a museum can use either a personal digital assistant (PDA) or a mobile phone with WLAN connecting capabilities to receive detailed descriptions of the artifacts at each exhibition point (Khan & Kellner, 2004).

An increasing number of firms are trying to deliver highly targeted campaigns to users using a GPS-enabled application that connects consumers to local businesses, people, restaurants, and movie theaters at the moment they want to buy or acquire products or services (Market Watch, 2011a). According to a recent industry report, eMarketer (2008) estimates that there will be over 63 million users of location-based services worldwide in 2011, and 486 million in 2012. At the same time, rapid advances in mobile Internet make consumers increasingly *situation aware*. Situation awareness can be defined as consumers' "perception of the elements of the environment within a volume of time and space, the comprehension of their meaning and the projection of their status in the near future" (Endsley, 1988, p. 97). In his seminal work, Belk (1975) proposed five situational variables that may influence consumer behavior, including physical and social surroundings. These situational variables seem very relevant to the concept of ubiquity, because LBSs are often dependent on circumstantial conditions and expectations.

The information obtained and delivered by LBS is not limited to spatial data, because maps may not necessarily be a required response. Instead, the information is more likely to include text, voice, diagrams, images (satellite, aerial, and terrestrial), video clips, and virtual reality scenes. The range of services offered by LBS includes:

1. Navigation: identifying appropriate and shortest routes for a vehicle to drive from a starting point to a destination.
2. Wayfinding: finding one's orientation in a given situation and discovering shortest routes and best mode of transport from a starting point to a destination.
3. Work-related fulfillment: tracking and updating orders related to deliveries, inspections, and data collection.
4. Proximity information: requesting, retrieving, or updating business, personal, and social user-solicited information, such as travel information, museum guides, weather forecasts, traffic conditions, train/flight schedules, ticket availability, and so on.
5. Emergency responses: transmitting urgent information related to accidents, interruptions of essential services, and natural disasters.
6. Real-time tracking: monitoring health status and locating vehicle fleets, business associates, social contacts, or family members.
7. Entertainment: enabling location-based games and alternate reality games (ARGs).

Wayfinding

Much research in LBS has focused on the nature of cognitive maps as internal spatial representations as well as how they are developed and how information for performing spatial activities is retrieved from them. When encountering a new environment, people are likely to need a range of information for completing spatial tasks. One of the most frequently encountered spatial tasks is finding a route and moving toward a destination. This behavior is called wayfinding (or navigation), and it involves multilevel cognitive processing. Wayfinding is the purposeful, directed, and motivated means for traveling from a point of origin to a given destination, and can be formally defined as "a consistent use and organization of definite sensory cues from the external environment" (Lynch, 1960). It involves selecting and following pathways through an existing network by which users can update information on traffic congestion, rerouting suggestions, and the best route to the destination (Allen, 1999; Golledge, 1999). In successful wayfinding, we first need to identify our current location (self-location) and then decide on the direction we are taking (orientation). On this basis, we then need to plan which route is the best (route selection) and follow this route to the destination (execution). In all these stages, we access stored knowledge about the surrounding space (internal representations) or refer to navigational aids such as maps (external representations). According to Xia, Packer, and Dong (2009), there are four important attributes of movement in wayfinding: *a route of motion* (points and lines), *the velocity of motion* (direction and speed), *time parameters related to movement* (arrival or departure time, duration of stay), and *the mode of movement or motion* (for example, by walking or through mechanized transport such as car or bus).

Wayfinding has been studied in various fields of information technology, environmental psychology, and urban systems, among others. In terms of navigational aids, various presentation formats of spatial information have been introduced, including verbal navigational directions, static maps, interactive maps, 3-D visualizations, animations, and virtual environments (Montello, Waller, Hegarty, & Richardson, 2004). Coors, Elting, Kray, and Laakso (2005) conducted a comparative study between 2-D maps and 3-D visualizations to find which is more effective as a means of presenting route instructions on mobile devices. Their findings suggest that 2-D maps enabled the respondents to locate their positions and to reach destinations more quickly than did 3-D visualizations. Similarly, Dillemuth (2005) found that an aerial photograph yielded faster travel speed and fewer navigation errors than a generalized map for a mobile navigational device.

As a wide variety of smartphones has proliferated, the number of tourism applications has increased. For example, TripAdvisor can now be used in iPhones or Androids (see Figure 7.1). Users can choose a location-based "Near Me" option to find hotels, restaurants, or any other entertainment activities that take place nearby. When users find "Coral Gables Merrick House and Gardens," pressing the "Get Direction" icon automatically brings users to that location on a Google interactive map, indicating the distance and time it requires. This is most likely one of the features that did not exist in previous versions of smartphones, with which users can experience truly ubiquitous function.

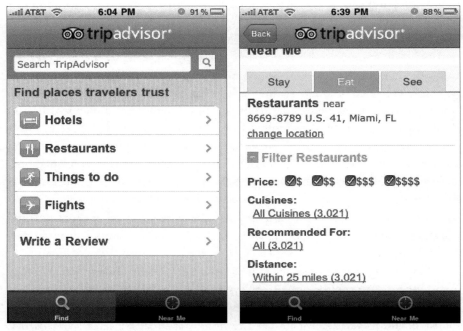

Fig. 7.1. TripAdvisor for Smartphone. Source: TripAdvisor (2011). Used by permission.

Bluetooth hotspot

Bluetooth is a short-range radio interface technology that provides wireless connectivity in a relatively short range. As shown in Table 7.1, there are three types of connectivity, from Class 1 (designed operating range 100 m) to Class 3 (1 m), with throughput up to 723.2 Kbps, or 2.1 Mbps using the globally available 2.4 GHz radio band. Each device can communicate simultaneously with up to seven other devices to form wireless personal area networks (WPANs) on a temporary and changing basis, commonly referred to as *piconets*. A piconet is composed of two or more Bluetooth devices in close physical proximity that operate on the same channel using the same frequency-hopping sequence. An example of a piconet is a Bluetooth-based connection between a cellular phone and a Bluetooth-enabled ear bud.

TABLE 7.1. Bluetooth Device Classes of Power Management

Type	Power	Power level	Designed operating range	Sample devices
Class 1	High	100 mW	Up to 100 meters	AC-powered devices (USB dongles, access points)
Class 2	Medium	2.5 mW	Up to 10 meters	Battery-powered devices (mobile devices, Bluetooth adapters, smart card readers)
Class 3	Low	1 mW	Up to 1 meter	Battery-powered devices (Bluetooth adapters)

Source: Bluetooth (2010)

Bluetooth piconets are often established on a temporary and changing basis, and this offers communication flexibility and scalability between mobile devices. Unlike a WLAN, which is comprised of both wireless user stations and access points, Bluetooth networks are comprised of wireless stations only. A Bluetooth station can be any Bluetooth-enabled device. Bluetooth-enabled devices automatically locate each other and form networks on a temporary, random basis. Some key benefits of Bluetooth technology are shown in Table 7.2.

TABLE 7.2. Key Benefits of Bluetooth

Key benefit	Description
Cable replacement	Bluetooth technology replaces a variety of cables, such as those traditionally used for peripheral devices (e.g., mouse and keyboard connections), printers, and wireless headsets and ear buds that interface with personal computers (PCs) or mobile telephones.
Ease of file sharing	A Bluetooth-enabled device can form a piconet to support file-sharing capabilities with other Bluetooth devices, such as laptops.
Wireless synchronization	Bluetooth provides automatic synchronization between Bluetooth-enabled devices. For example, Bluetooth allows synchronization of contact information contained in electronic address books and calendars.
Internet connectivity	A Bluetooth device with Internet connectivity can share that access with other Bluetooth devices. For example, a laptop can use a Bluetooth connection to have a mobile phone establish a dial-up connection, so that the laptop can access the Internet through the phone.

Source: Jansen and Scarfone (2008)

There have been several versions of Bluetooth, including Version 3.0 High Speed (HS), adopted in April 2009, and Version 2.1 Enhanced Data Rate (EDR), adopted in July 2007. The most recent Version 4.0 was adopted in June 2010 and includes Classic Bluetooth, Bluetooth high speed and Bluetooth low energy protocols. Bluetooth high speed is based on Wi-Fi, and Classic Bluetooth consists of legacy Bluetooth protocols (Bluetooth, 2010). The v4.0 Bluetooth Core Specification features (1) ultra-low peak, average, and idle mode power consumption (as little as 10% of the energy used by the classic Bluetooth version); (2) ability to run for years on standard coin-cell batteries; (3) low cost; (4) multi-vendor interoperability; and (5) enhanced range.

Bluetooth technology has been integrated into many types of business and consumer devices, including smartphones. One industry research report estimates that there were nearly 3 billion Bluetooth devices in the marketplace in 2010. Probably the industry in which Bluetooth technology has been most appreciated is tourism. In many parts of the world, airports have been using mobile technology to attract more tourists. For example, in Ljubljana, Slovenia, Jože Pučnik Airport has partnered with the Slovenian Tourist Board, Aerodrom Ljubljana, and Creativ Interaktiv to provide numerous travel benefits to tourists via Bluetooth. Arriving passengers are invited to turn on their mobile phone Bluetooth feature as they are bused from the airplane to the terminal, and again as they pass through customs to the baggage claim area called the "Bluetooth Zone." If Bluetooth is activated, the travelers are asked whether they want to receive tourism information for Slovenia. If they indicate "yes," they receive a free SMS text message with instructions to download the information, in both Slovene and English, including travel tips, recommended tourist attractions and events, and mobile coupons from partner organizations.

Similar services are offered in many places throughout the world. In Vancouver, Canada, BlueZones combine Wi-Fi and Bluetooth to send a variety of content to mobile devices. Within 30 meters of each Bluetooth hotspot, users receive a text invitation, which they can accept or reject, to download and view a short video clip promoting local tourism events and schedules. In the U.K., visitors to Aviemore and the Cairngorms in the Scottish Highlands can access tourist information using three Bluetooth terminals. At Raglan Castle, a late medieval castle located in the county of Monmouthshire in southeast Wales, local tourism officials have been distributing audio files to visitors' mobile phones using Bluetooth on a trial basis. According to one user, Tom, at Lexemetch.com, "As I walked through the entrance I simply made my phone discoverable, waited a few seconds for the MP3 to download, then started listening to a guided tour of the castle."

From a practitioner's standpoint, Bluetooth is an efficient data collection tool. For example, Manchester Airport in the U.K. uses a Bluetooth-enabled measurement gathered from traffic data on passengers' mobile phones and PDAs in order to track wait times and restructure queue dwell times (Sharsky, 2009). Approximately 6% of passengers in airport security lines have a Bluetooth-enabled mobile phone, PDA, MP3 player, or other personal device that is detectable (DBIS, 2010). The data collected from these devices can be used for a mathematical analysis of waiting in lines called Queueing Theory. Operations researchers use this technique to estimate the wait time for many locations or situations, including grocery stores, call centers, telecommunications, computer networks, and health care (Sharsky, 2009). In order to ensure privacy, firms record only passengers' Bluetooth signals, not personal information.

In the Yorkshire Dales National Park, visitors who stand on the Bluetooth hotspot outside the National Park Centre can follow the step-by-step instructions posted in the window (Figure 7.2) to download park information. This free facility is the latest attempt by the Yorkshire Dales National Park Authority to reduce the number of panels located in the National Park that give visitors information about the immediate area. Similarly, the Grassington National Park Centre in the Yorkshire Dales installed a Bluetooth unit that will enable people to download "Discover Grassington" (a package of information about the area that includes self-guided river and village walks) onto their mobile phones, laptops, or other equipment, even when the building is closed.

Fig. 7.2. Yorkshire Dales National Park's Bluetooth Information Service. Source: Culture24 (2009).

By activating the Bluetooth on their mobile phones, visitors at Disneyland Paris can find out how long the waiting time is for a particular ride or find out the starting times for the park's shows. The Bluetooth terminals are indicated on the park program and are situated in the waiting line for Crush's Coaster, in the Twilight Zone Tower of Terror, beside the information panel at the exit of Studio 1, and in the En Coulisse restaurant. As visitors walk by these terminals, they receive an alert indicating that they can receive information via Bluetooth. Then they can accept or reject the invitation. Eric Cosset, parks operation director for Disneyland Paris, said, "Our position as Europe's leading tourist destination requires that our level of services be increasingly performing, in order to guarantee a quality experience for our guests."

Mobile museum guidance

One of the objectives of mobile personal museum guidance is improving the effectiveness of the users' museum experience. Mobile personal museum guidance has two major advantages over current alternatives such as audio tours. First, communication is more efficient, with richer content through multimedia presentations, including images, video, audio, text, and computer graphics. Second, museum operators benefit from lower maintenance and acquisition costs for their presentation technology, since the visitors themselves provide the end-devices.

In a seminal work, Evans and Sterry (1999) explained an interactive multimedia application called the GEMISIS 2000 project of the University of Salford, U.K., and offered some preliminary findings. In this project, the audio guides were combined with CD-ROM and interactive multimedia kiosks in a portable computer. An evaluation showed that while portable computers enhanced visitors' learning and increased the time they spent in the gallery, the size and weight of the computer were problematic. To compensate for this shortcoming, Personal Digital Assistants (PDAs) have been introduced into museums.

The PEACH (Personal Experience with Active Cultural Heritage) project is an effort financed by the Autonomous Province of Trento, Italy, and is coordinated by ITC-irst, in collaboration with DFKI, the German Institute for Artificial Intelligence Research, the Cybernetic Institute of Napoli, CNR, the Superintendent of Ercolano and Pompei Excavations, Columbia University in New York City, the National Research Council of Canada, and the University of Padova. The project applied the idea of using cinematographic techniques for presenting details of artworks in a multimedia guide prototype, aiming at personalizing the visitors' experience (Alfaro et al., 2004). A first prototype of the PEACH was introduced at Torre Aquila, a frescoed tower at the Buonconsiglio Castle in Trento, Italy. The main tourist attraction is "The Cycle of the Months," a Gothic masterpiece consisting of 11 panels and painted in the 15th century.

The multimedia guide, consisting of audio commentary accompanied by a sequence of images on a PDA, automatically detects the position of the visitor by means of infrared beamers placed in front of each panel. In a later guide prototype, the PEACH automatically produced video clips on the mobile device using a life-like character either as an anchorman or a presenter who accompanies the visitor throughout the visit (Rocchi & Zancanaro, 2004). Additional prototypes focused on providing easy-to-use interfaces that allow users to signal their interest in the topic being presented and support better personalization of the presentation delivered (Goren-Bar et al., 2005). As shown in Figure 7.3, Buonconsiglio Castle offers a user-friendly mobile audio guide. Users first access and choose one of the 11 panels. According to the panel chosen, the audio explanation begins, while a video shows a sequence of images.

Similarly, the PEACH has been implemented at the Saarbrucken Völklinger Hütte Museum of Metallurgic Industry in southwest Germany. The museum's home page includes a link to a special service for its visitors. Before visiting the Völklinger Hütte and its exhibitions, visitors can download the audio guides that can be transferred to a mobile device or MP3 player through Bluetooth, IR, or USB interface. In the Netherlands, the Rijksmuseum Amsterdam, or Dutch State Museum, teamed up with the University of Amsterdam to develop the CHIP (Cultural Heritage Information Personalization) project in order to enhance access to digital museum collections. The technology involves an RFID-reader-enabled device and allows users to access information inside the museum and on the museum's Web site and then be synchronized with the servers on demand. The user profile created on the Web site and the tour data (both in XML) can be downloaded from the CHIP server to the mobile device for use during the physical museum tour. When the museum tour is over, the user data can be synchronized with the user profile on the server.

While IR beamers, RFID tags, and GPS have been used to determine the position of a museum visitor and provide additional information (Bombara, Cali, & Santoro, 2003; RFID Journal, 2004), some researchers claim that these approaches are either too expensive or impractical in performing quick recognition and classification of a large number of objects with mobile devices (Föckler et al., 2005). There is a trend toward techniques that enable visitors to recognize exhibits and works of art reliably and directly from, and only with, mobile devices.

One of the most successful mobile object recognition systems is called PhoneGuide. In this system, all image-processing tasks are done directly through

Fig. 7.3. CHIP Mobile Museum Guide.

Note: From left to right: (a) Users can first consult a museum map; then (b) enter a tour selection page with a configuration screen; (c) choose a tour sequence; and (d) access a detailed guide of the artworks. An online demo is available at: http://www.chip-project.org/demo/mobileguide/ (an ID is required). Source: Wang et al. (2009).

the phone itself, rather than on remote servers. This all but eliminates the need for network connectivity and reduces online access costs. In the PhoneGuide, visitors merely take a photograph of an exhibit, and, using this, the classifiers carry out image classification. After classification, a probability-sorted list of objects is presented on the phone's screen. The correct object can be selected with a minimum number of clicks in order to retrieve the corresponding multimedia information. Each sensor box includes a Bluetooth chip to transmit its data, including a unique ID, to the mobile phones that should be located in its signal range. Each device can know its own rough position within the museum by analyzing all detectable sensor boxes. Based on this information, the classifier selector chooses a classifier optimized for recognizing only the objects that are located in the proximity of the user. In practice, only a small number of objects need to be distinguished from each other, while an arbitrary number of objects can be recognized with a suitable number of signal cells (Bruns, Brombach, & Bimber, 2008).

Bruns and colleagues (2008) implemented the PhoneGuide in the Museum of the City of Weimar, Germany. The PhoneGuide uses camera-equipped mobile phones for on-device object recognition in combination with pervasive tracking. This system was tested in the museum, which displays a large and varying palette of artifacts ranging from furniture to pictures in 15 different rooms on 2 floors.

Mobile health monitoring

The increased need for real-time data management and the advances in mobile communication technology are developing markets for a new form of data management systems in the health care industry. Medical reference literature, electronic patient records, and emergency surgery information can now be exchanged via smartphone. For example, Eponyms App is the iPhone version of Andrew Yee's huge eponym database consisting of over 1,600 medical eponyms. Pedi Stat is a quick iPhone reference for RNs, paramedics, physicians, and other health care professionals treating pediatric patients in the emergency or critical care environment. With just a few taps, users have access to all necessary data, including specific medication dosages and equipment sizes based on age, date of birth, weight, length, or height.

The program is especially useful for (1) airway interventions, including endotracheal tube sizes, depth, intubation medication dosages, ventilator settings, and sedation; (2) cardiac resuscitation data management, including weight-specific dosages for resuscitation medications, cardioversion, and defibrillation; and (3) management of hypoglycemia, including age-specific dextrose concentrations, among others. Epocrates App is available in both iPhone and Android phones and offers (1) drug information related to thousands of brand-name and generic OTC drugs, with indications, contraindications, retail pricing, and mechanism of action; (2) a pill identifier based on the color, shape, or imprint code; (3) a drug interaction checker for up to 30 drugs at a time; (4) drug monographs and health plan formularies; (5) clinical articles; (6) content updates and medical news; and (7) infectious disease treatment guides, among others.

Along with these practical smartphone applications, health monitoring with a mobile device on a more comprehensive scale has been receiving increased interest among both patients and physicians. The basic idea is that persons can monitor their physiological and psychological parameters by themselves at home using medical devices. This system could be especially useful in the management of chronic disorders or health problems; for example, for high blood pressure, diabetes, anorexia nervosa, chronic pain, or severe obesity (Korhonen, Pärkkä & van Gils, 2003). Health monitoring with a mobile device could also work as a control and feedback system to help prevent disease. While a patient's PC or PDA can double as a personal home server, a mobile device is more suitable because of its portability.

The objective of mobile health monitoring is twofold. First, it provides health care services to anyone, overcoming the constraints of place, time, and character. Second, it helps citizens participate more actively in their own health care. In many cases, people with medical issues are unaware, unwilling, or unable to regularly go to a physician. Obesity, high blood pressure, irregular heartbeat, and diabetes are examples of such common health problems. In particular, cardiovascular disease is the leading cause of death and accounts for approximately 30% of all deaths worldwide. Those who have such diseases are normally advised to visit their doctors periodically for routine medical checkups. But if we can provide them with a more personalized and flexible means through which they can get the same medical feedback, it will save valuable time, satisfy their desire for personal control over their own health, and lower the cost of long-term medical care (Shahriyar et al., 2009).

A Body Sensor Network (BSN) uses biosensors as a key component to control patients' health conditions. A BSN consists of miniaturized, low-power, and noninvasive or invasive wireless biosensors, which are seamlessly placed on or implanted in the body in order to provide an adaptable and smart health care system (Ullah et al., 2008). A biosensor is "a chemical sensing device in which a biologically derived recognition entity is coupled to a transducer, to allow the quantitative development of some complex biochemical parameter" (Aware Home Research Initiative, 2010). The device consists of two parts: bioelement and sensor-element. A bioelement recognizes a specific chemical constituent that is undergoing analysis, which can be an enzyme, antibody, living cell, or tissue. A sensor-element converts the bio-molecule change into an electrical signal, which may be electric current or electric potential. The biosensors can have a variety of biomedical and industry applications, including glucose level monitoring, ECG sensing, pulse measurement, blood pressure monitoring, cell morphology monitoring, and so on.

One of the practical BSN applications is the wearable body sensor network (WBSN). WBSN is formed with wearable or implantable biosensors in a patient's body. These sensors collect necessary readings from the patient. For each organ, a group of sensors will send their readings to the group leader. The group leaders communicate with each other, and they send the aggregated information to the central controller. The central controller is responsible for transmitting patient data to the personal computer or cell phone/PDA. It has been suggested by van Halteren and colleagues (2004) that the tissue medium acts as a channel through which the information is sent as electromagnetic radio frequency. The central controller of the WBSN communicates with the Patients Personal Home Server (PPHS) using any of the two wireless protocols: Bluetooth or WLAN. Bluetooth can be used for short-range distances between the central controller and PPHS. For example, Bluetooth version 4.0 could include wireless heart-rate sensors, pedometers, and GPS locators for athletes and health monitoring. WLAN can be used to allow more distance between them.

A refinement of BSN has yielded a Body Area Network (BAN). A BAN is sometimes referred to as a Body Area Sensor Network (BASN) or, in short, a Body Sensor Network (BSN). A BAN can be defined as "a collection of (inter) communicating devices which are worn on the body, providing an integrated set of personalized services to the user" (WWRF, 2001). As such, the BSN remains the most thought-out application of BAN. However, BAN technology is quite flexible, and there are many potential uses for it in addition to BSNs, including mobile health monitoring. In mobile health monitoring, a patient is wearing a BAN consisting of one or more specialized sensing devices and a Mobile Base Unit (MBU) (Hanson, Powell, & Barth, 2009; Wac et al., 2009). A sensing device may monitor a patient's vital signs in a particular area (e.g., cardiac arrhythmia, respiration insufficiency, chronic neck-shoulder pain, epilepsy). A sensing device may also be in the form of a button that can be pressed by the patient in an emergency situation, or a sensor (e.g., a GPS receiver) that can determine the location of a patient. The MBU is the central unit of a BAN, usually based on a mobile phone or PDA platform. The MBU has three functions: (1) collection and (time) synchronization of sensor data, (2) data processing, and (3) transfer of (processed) data to a remote application backend server in a health care facility. Once the sensor data are transferred to the backend server, it is available to other applications, for example, data retrieval, data visualization, or medical decision support applications (Jones et al., 2006).

A BAN incorporates a set of devices that perform some specific functions and communicate. Communication between the nodes and the MBU is called *intra-BAN communication*. Intra-BAN communication may be transported over a wired or a wireless medium. Wired options include copper wires, optical fibers, and various "wearable computing" solutions. Wireless options include infrared light, microwave, radio, and even skin conductivity. Communication between the MBU and the backend server is referred to as *extra-BAN communication*. Extra-BAN communication may be based on wireless technologies including Bluetooth, WLAN, GSM, GPRS, and UMTS.

Regulatory requirements must always be met when adopting mobile health monitoring. Devices must not disturb patients, either directly or indirectly. In addition, the wireless transmission of data must not harm the surrounding tissues and the chronic functioning of the patients' bodies, and the power used for these devices must be non-malignant. Safety design must be a fundamental consideration of biomedical sensor development, even in the earliest stages. Because it is conceivable that researchers could perform immoral and dangerous tests and trials with devices, it is critical that these testing operations be carefully regulated (Khan, Hussain, & Kwak, 2009).

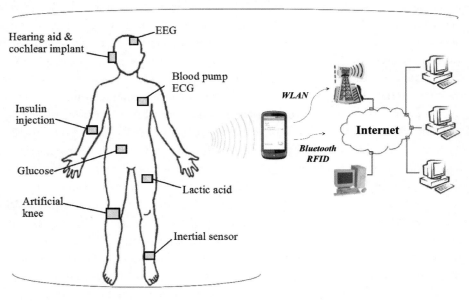

Fig. 7.4. Basic Model of Mobile Health Monitoring with a Body Area Network.

Note: EEG is an acronym for electroencephalogram, which is a diagnostic tool to detect problems in the electrical activity of the brain. ECG (or EKG) is an acronym for electrocardiogram, which is a diagnostic tool that records the electrical activity of the heart. Source: Own elaboration.

Finally, mobile health, or mHealth, delivered through cellular technologies, is part of a movement toward health services tailored to individuals, and health notifications and data geared to public health officials and researchers. Mobile phones in particular are increasingly used to inform health care practitioners and the public about infectious disease outbreaks. For individuals, mHealth technologies can monitor vital signs and even provide risk assessments, medication regimens, and doctor appointment reminders (Condayan, 2010).

Information privacy concerns

A recent industry survey found that 62% of marketers used some form of mobile marketing for their brands in 2010, and an additional 26% intended to do so in 2011. Perhaps more significantly, research suggests that LBS will account for at least US$10 billion in marketing revenue by 2016 (Desai et al., 2011). This dramatic growth raises a serious concern over LBS-based information privacy considerations.

A Google search of "LBS" and "privacy" results in 118 million hits. It is completely unethical to track and monitor someone without his or her consent. The dilemma with LBS, however, is that its primary function is as a tracking device. In a 2011 survey conducted by PluGGd.in, consumers indicated that privacy is their primary concern (38%), with more of a concern expressed by older users than by younger users. Consumers do not entirely trust mobile app stores, as only 25% of respondents believe that applications purchased from app stores protect their privacy.

The concept of information privacy deals with the rights of those people whose information is shared. Westin (1967, p. 7) defines information privacy as "the claim of individuals, groups, or institutions to determine for themselves when, how, and to what extent information about them is communicated to others." Information privacy becomes a prominent issue in computer-mediated communication, because the interactive process can collect significant amounts of personal information and store it indefinitely for later use. Needless to say, mobile communication is no exception. In the context of mobile marketing, however, information privacy has not been explored much, except in earlier research that focused on consumers' acceptance of permission-based advertising.

From the industry side, the MMA released a set of global privacy guidelines for mobile marketers in 2008 (MediaPost, 2008). The new Global Code of Conduct broadens the scope of the privacy rules that the MMA issued in 2007 for the U.S. market, with input from its Latin American, Asian-Pacific and European, Middle Eastern, and African chapters. The code encompasses voluntary guidelines in five categories:

- Notice—Informing the user of the products and services offered, or the marketers' identity, and the essential terms and conditions utilized between the marketer and the user's mobile device.
- Choice and Consent—Respecting the right of the user to accept or reject mobile messages.
- Customization and Constraint—Ensuring that data collected are limited to information that benefits the user in the form of product and service enhancements, contests, requested information, entertainment, or discounts. Treating information responsibly, sensitively, and in compliance with applicable law.
- Security—Implementing necessary technical, administrative, and physical procedures to protect user data from unauthorized use, alteration, disclosure, distribution, or access.
- Enforcement and Accountability—Complying with the MMA Privacy Code of Conduct and following relevant MMA guidelines, including the U.S. Consumer Best Practice guidelines.

Until the code can be effectively enforced by a third-party organization, mobile marketers are expected to use evaluations of their practices to certify compliance with the code. The privacy guidelines came a week after the MMA updated its consumer best practices rules and almost 2 months after it issued new technical guidelines on mobile banner and text ads.

However, some advocacy groups say the emerging mobile ad business needs more than voluntary standards on privacy. The Center for Digital Democracy and the U.S. Public Interest Research Group plan to file an amended complaint with the Federal Trade Commission (FTC) on behavioral targeting in general, but encompassing mobile marketing. Jeff Chester, founder and executive director of the Center for Digital Democracy, argues: "The FTC has to proactively ensure [that] consumers control their information and that the mobile marketing 'ecosystem' is an opt-in, fully transparent, user-controlled mobile system." The FCC already prohibits marketers from sending text message ads to consumers without their consent, but some other types of nascent mobile ads—such as WAP (wireless application protocol) banners or search ads—are not similarly restricted. The Privacy Committee of the MMA North American chapter developed the code of conduct with participation from mobile companies, content providers, and advertisers including Ad Infuse, AOL, Microsoft, Procter & Gamble, Verizon Wireless, Qualcomm, and Yahoo! Nonetheless, despite such progress in privacy guidelines in mobile marketing practices, there has apparently been a forgotten area. In April 2011, ABC News (2011) reported that, according to researchers, some Apple iPhone and iPad owners had their locations tracked by their devices. In another news report by ABC (2011), a security researcher discovered that Android phones, powered by Google's mobile operating system, store users' geographic information in a similar fashion.

In 2011, the MMA posted Desai and colleagues' (2011) in-depth review of U.S. public authorities' concerns over LBS-based marketing. The U.S. Congress, the FTC, and the FCC have developed a special interest in the marketing practices that LBS providers employ. For example, Senator Al Franken (D-MN), chairman of the Judiciary Committee's new Subcommittee on Privacy, Technology and the Law, recently introduced legislation intending to regulate conduct in the LBS market and summarized the need for federal intervention as follows: "Geolocation technology gives us incredible benefits, but the same information that allows emergency responders to locate us when we're in trouble is not necessarily information all of us want to share with the rest of the world."

Summary

Location-based services (LBSs) enable users to take full advantage of spatial information and thus have been widely used in some industries, including tourism and health care. Technologies such as the global positioning system (GPS), Bluetooth, and other wireless technology are used to provide, update, and monitor users' location-based information. The chapter describes various LBS applications in tourism, including place marketing, wayfinding, and Bluetooth hotspots. In particular, the importance of place marketing is increasing in popular tourist destinations for better branding practices. The chapter also introduces a mobile-based health monitoring system that employs a wearable body sensor network (WBSN). Here, LBS can be a useful tool for remotely controlling patients' chronic health problems, including heart disease and diabetes. In closing, an important issue associated with LBS, information privacy concerns, is explicated.

8

Mobile Payment AND Security

The mobile payments sector is booming at the moment, with companies such as Google, Intuit, Square, and—of course—the eBay-backed PayPal all competing for a share of customer transactions. On July 13, 2011, PayPal unveiled a new peer-to-peer payment functionality that allows Android users to pay each other by tapping two NFC-enabled devices together. Likewise, on September 20, 2011, Google Wallet was launched in the United States with NFC-preinstalled Google Nexus S smartphones.

Goods and services purchased via smartphone have to be paid for. Thus, the acceptance of mobile marketing would largely depend on the availability, efficiency, usability, and security of payment. Regardless of what services are offered, unless their acquisition and settlement are simple and safe enough, few consumers would actually purchase the services. In this regard, as innovative instruments have been gradually but steadily developed, mobile payment offers an important opportunity for retailing channels. In earlier days, fixed phone billing was modified to include mobile telephone charges. Later, mobile telephone billing was modified to charge for various mobile services. Nowadays, the mobile telephone offers a payment solution to facilitate micropayment, while enabling a cashless alternative for transactions at the point of sale (POS). This chapter addresses the conceptual and technological development of mobile payment and its application in various sectors.

Academic research on mobile payment services dates back to the late 1990s. A recent review of the literature on mobile payments between 1999 and 2006 identified 73 publications, among which 30 and 43 were, respectively, empirical and conceptual papers. As many as 57 were published in conference proceedings, while only 16 appeared in academic journals. The majority of the empirical studies address consumer adoption of mobile payment, while technological issues are predominant in both types of research. This may imply that mobile payment is mainly a technological issue, which would affect the availability of payment options with a mobile device.

Payment as a social contract

Before conducting any financial transaction, people need to believe the system is well accepted socially, and therefore trustworthy. In explaining how society organizes itself in accordance with the mutually beneficial principles of justice, social contract theory provides a rationale for the historically important notion that legitimate state authority must be derived from the consent of the governed (Macneil, 1974). Social contracts comprise a broad class of implied agreements by which people form nations and maintain social order. Thus, social contract theory attempts to explain why rational and impartial people voluntarily give up their freedom of action in a natural state ("natural rights") to obtain the benefits provided by the formation of social structures (Macneil, 1974).

According to this theory, the nature of a contract evolves from four principles of society: specialization of labor, exchange, choice, and awareness of the future. As labor has become more specialized over time, persons and companies no longer produce for themselves everything they need in order to thrive; instead, they must depend on exchanges with others for products and services. Exchanges that involve the promise of future benefits represent contracts. Furthermore, the level of choice that people and/or companies have among a range of exchanges reveals the extent of the freedom they enjoy. However, without awareness of the future, a contract that defines such exchanges is not worth pursuing, because consciousness of the future determines the need for a contract (Macneil, 1974).

Contracts entail a continuum, from discrete to relational. Discrete contracts are short-term, single transactions between unrelated parties, whereas relational contracts involve long-term, dynamic transactions with related parties. These relationships are separate from the exchange of the goods. Therefore, in a mobile marketing context, firms are required to establish social contracts, that is, implicit, noncommercial relationships characterized by multiple transactions with their customers (Milne & Gordon, 1994). In exchange, customers offer their personal commitment (i.e., purchase), but if firms break from the expected pattern of behavior, consumers believe their rights have been violated (Milne & Gordon, 1994). In relation to mobile-based financial transactions, the relationships between mobile users and mobile marketers may need to be stronger, thus establishing a more explicit social contract as compared with other e-commerce formats, for two reasons. First, a mobile device is often perceived as a very personal communication tool and thus requires a stronger tie between remitter and recipients. Second, mobile transactions often deal with limited tangibility in terms of product display, and stronger trust is therefore needed.

When mobile users partake of financial services with their devices, they expect their rights to be respected by the provider. This expectation—to receive the promised benefits in exchange for a payment commitment—reflects the concept of trust. When parties engage in a contractual relationship, one party must assume that the other will take responsibility for its promises. As Golembiewski and McConkie (1975, p. 131) state, "There is no single variable which so thoroughly influences interpersonal and group behavior as does trust." Moorman, Deshpandé, and Zaltman (1993) conceptualize trust as a willingness to reply to an exchange partner in whom one has confidence, grounded in Rotter's (1971) classic definition of trust as one party's general expectation that it can rely on another.

Trust has been proposed as a multidimensional concept. Early research on e-commerce (e.g., Sheehan & Hoy, 1999) indicated that as concern about privacy increases, users register for Web sites less frequently and provide incomplete information, possibly because they have less trust in the Web site. That is, trust becomes manifest in the willingness of a party to be vulnerable to the actions of another. This is based on the expectation that the other will perform a particular action important to the truster, irrespective of its ability to monitor or control that other party (Mayer, Davis, & Schoorman, 1995).

Mobile payment system

A mobile payment system is comprised of four principal players: customer, merchant/content provider, payment service provider (PSP), and trusted third party (TTP). (See Figure 8.1.)

When a mobile user wants to purchase content with a mobile device, this user first becomes a customer and needs to register in a PSP to initialize the purchasing process. The merchant forwards the purchase request to the PSP that is responsible for the payment process. A PSP can be a network operator, a bank, a credit card company, or an independent payment vendor. Second, the PSP inquires about the authentication to the TTP that is responsible for the authorization of the payment request. The TTP issues the service certificate for a given account, which can be associated with monetary value or personal data. A TTP can be a network operator, a bank, a credit card company, or an intermediary. The TTP identifies the mobile user, for example, with a PIN code, and completes the authorization so that the merchant can deliver the content. In many cases, mobile network operators, banks, or intermediaries may function simultaneously as the TTP, PSP, and/or content provider, in which case the model can be reduced to only three or even two players.

There are different security dimensions that need to be distinguished in terms of network transmission: authentication, confidentiality, integrity, and non-repudiation. The authentication concerns how parties' identities are verified in a communication. Obviously, we need to ensure that the verified users are the persons they claim to be. Confidentiality deals with the limited disclosure of the message. That is, the sender of the message allows only the intended recipient to read its content. Integrity is about ensuring the consistency and accuracy between what was sent and what was received. Intentional, ill-natured, or accidental alteration of the message must be prevented or stopped in a communication process. Finally, non-repudiation is concerned with the mechanisms that guarantee a false claim—the person who made a transaction cannot say later that he or she did not. Among alternatives, cryptography[1] is one of the most widely accepted mechanisms that satisfy all these dimensions.

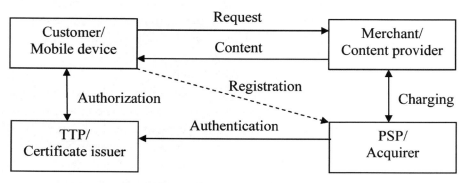

Fig. 8.1. Mobile Payment Model. Source: Hassinen, Hyppönen, & Trichina (2007).

Classification of mobile payment

Mobile payment can be defined as "wireless transactions of monetary value from one party to another where a mobile device (such as a mobile phone, smartphone, or personal digital assistant (PDA) is used in order to initiate, activate, and/or confirm the payments for goods, services, and/or bills" (Dahlberg et al., 2008; Hassinen et al., 2007). Mobile payments can be classified into various categories. For example, transactions can vary according to the settlement method, which can be pre-paid, post-paid, or pay-now. In addition, the type of goods purchased can be either virtual or real. Furthermore, the value of payments can be pico-, micro-, or macro-payments. Finally, the environment in which a mobile payment is carried out can be characterized by the distance between the settlement and the payee, including remote (traditional e-commerce transactions with a mobile device), local (credit card payment at a physical POS), or proximity (payment at vending machines or self-service transactions with contactless payment function). From the technological perspective, there are competing alternatives that are mainly either physical (SIM WIM, dual slot, external card reader, etc.) or virtual (SMS, USSD, WAP, RFID, Bluetooth, etc.).

SAT-based system

Customer authentication is one of the key issues in mobile payment, because a mobile device is highly personal and thus susceptible to sensitive transactions. In GSM, every mobile phone is equipped with a removable element called a Subscriber Identity Module (SIM), which is a tamper-resistant, removable microprocessor chip-card containing essential information (i.e. identifiers, keys and algorithms) for a mobile network operator to authenticate a subscriber (Jansen and Scarfone, 2008). Mobile users can store all their vital information in a SIM. Essentially, it is a repository that includes a user's authentication key and a PIN code that need to be entered to unlock the SIM.

To use a SIM as a trusted mode of mobile payment, the European Telecommunications Standards Institute developed a SIM Application Toolkit, a standard for authorizing payment transactions with GSM-enabled mobile phones. In order to authenticate a SIM, a so-called "challenge-response method" is used. With this method, the authentication center sends a random number to the SIM, which in turn combines this number with the user's authentication key using an authentication algorithm. This process stays on the SIM (or the smart card inserted in the mobile device), and the result—called "signed response"—is returned over the wireless link for comparison with the result obtained by the authentication center.

By matching the two values, the user is considered to be authenticated. In this authentication method, the mobile operation gains a strong position, because the SIM must be obtained when users open their mobile phone subscription with the mobile operator. However, the 3G or UMTS network system has brought several enhancements to the security features of the 2G or GSM network system, such as data integrity and protection against the false base station attack, which do not necessarily require a SIM.

NFC-based system

NFC, which we discussed in Chapter 5, is being used as a form of mobile payment with much more regularity. This is most likely due to the fact that its wireless connectivity technology enables simple and safe two-way interactions between electronic devices. NFC's communication interface allows consumers to perform contactless transactions, access digital content, and connect electronic devices with a single touch, within a short range of about 10 cm. This technology has drawn increasing attention since Google announced the NFC-based mobile wallet (Digital Transactions, 2011).

In this project, Google reached an agreement with Visa Inc., American Express Co., and Discover Financial Services to add their cards to the wallet, which had been limited to MasterCard Inc. since the product was unveiled in May 2011. This Google mobile wallet is part of the Nexus S 4G smartphone on the Sprint Nextel network, which can be used at any of the 144,000 U.S. merchant locations that accept contactless payments.

This payment method seems to have several benefits over the payment alternatives based on a SIM or bar code. First, NFC allows users to take advantage of time-space flexible discounts by receiving coupons and reading encoded posters in retail outlets at the point of sale. As an extension of Google Wallet, Google introduced mobile promotional programs with this technology called Google Offers and SingleTap. Google Offers features e-mail discount offers from local businesses. Google SingleTap is used when making payments with the Google Wallet—just as the name suggests, it requires only one tap to secure payment. Another benefit of Google Wallet is its addition of major payment entities including Visa, American Express, and Discover. With this, Google can compete with Isis, an NFC initiative backed by the country's largest mobile carriers, in terms of major payment networks represented for NFC payment. With these developments, Google Wallet will enable consumers to use a smartphone as a substitute for these credit cards by simply swiping their phone at the point of sale. This technology is similar to FeliCa, Sony's contactless RFID smart card system, which was launched in Japan in 2004.

In spite of these advantages, it remains to be seen whether U.S. consumers will embrace Google Wallet. In relation to this question, Ogilvy and Mather conducted a survey on the level of trust consumers have with mobile providers (ZDNet, 2011). The research firm engaged 500 subjects to test their trust of 11 providers, including Visa, MasterCard, American Express, PayPal, and Google. Respondents were able to choose any number of these providers, without limit, to indicate which one(s) they would trust to receive their mobile payment. According to the results, just under 20% of respondents said that they trust Google as a payment method. In contrast, 40% trusted Visa, while only 12% would trust Facebook as a mobile payment method. Apple led the list of consumer technology companies with a 23% trust rating.

Toward globalization of mobile payment systems

Mobile payment has entered a new era in which rapid innovations in financial technology require global standards. This trend is also consistent with an increasing number of consumers living, working, or traveling worldwide. There is a growing need for a system of instruments and rules that permits different methods and regulations in different geographical areas, such as credit and debit cards. Advances in mobile technology may allow more efficient and secure cross-border payment systems through the Internet. For example, in addition to the existing worldwide payment systems such as PayPal or iDeal, which allow users to send or receive payment in foreign currencies, NFC-based mobile payment may grow drastically as consumers' trust increases. However, the use of these payment systems with a mobile device may bring to light more security issues.

iPhone's App Store is no exception. This seemingly global platform has a strict policy that demands the registration of credit cards issued in the countries where users reside. Problems arise when users try to purchase and pay for goods or services in foreign countries. For example, imagine that you are thinking of purchasing a game that is only available in the United States, but you live in Japan and your credit card is issued there. The only option for completing this purchase is to buy a Visa or MasterCard prepaid card, which can be used in any App Store settlement. Some may argue that this payment restriction is unavoidable, given the increasing fraud in international credit card settlements, but we undoubtedly need a more flexible way to make payment. Otherwise, mobile payment transactions will be limited to the country of the user's residence, without any mobility.

Besides the NFC-based payment method, one alternative for international mobile payment could be the use of a SIM card. The advantage of this option is simplicity, since neither personal nor financial data are required for the settlement. For example, after the introduction of Apple's iPad, NTT DoCoMo announced it would sell SIM cards for other carriers, changing its traditional policy. This may alter the competitive picture painted by Japanese mobile carriers that have always been reluctant to be aligned with foreign competitors in global markets.

Security issues

Security issues constitute the most serious threat to mobile Internet services. There are more than 2 billion mobile phones in service today, a number that represents an enormous potential target for malicious mobile software. A mobile virus is an electronic virus that targets mobile phones or wireless-enabled PDAs. The number of such viruses has recently soared from 1 to over 200. This exponential increase mirrors what happened to PC viruses in the 2 years after the first computer virus was detected in 1986. Today more than 300 kinds of malware, such as worms, Trojan horses, other viruses, and spyware, have been unleashed against mobile devices worldwide.

Cell phone viruses primarily target three mobile operating systems: Symbian, Windows Mobile, and a third in use by NTT DoCoMo, one of the largest cell phone operators in Japan. This malicious software has destroyed files, forced phones to dial 911 or premium-rate phone numbers without the user's consent, and ruined handhelds with "denial-of-service attacks" in which the device gets so many inbound calls that it can't process all the traffic.

The first computer virus to attack mobile phones was "Timofonica," identified in 2000 in Spain, where customers of the phone company Movistar were hit with annoying computer-generated phone calls. The Timofonica virus was written using Microsoft's VBScript programming language and spread via e-mail by sending infected messages from affected computers. The worm sent itself to all addresses stored in a person's address book and delivered a message disparaging the Spanish telephone company Telefonica. In addition, the worm sent a text message to phone users. The worm randomly generated phone numbers targeting the "corio.movistar.net" SMS gate. Every time the worm was forwarded to a new address, it sent a new SMS message to a randomly selected number, thus bombarding people with SMS messages.

In early 2004, mobile phone users who knowingly downloaded an illegal version of the game Mosquitos to play on their handset were "infected" by a Trojan horse that sent costly SMS messages without the owner realizing it. This premium-rate SMS functionality was later found to be a botched copy-protection feature of the original manufacturer that prevented users from buying cheaper versions in different countries. However, this "virus alert" was spread all over the world, causing smartphone users on Symbian handsets to become seriously concerned. Mobile phones running the Windows Mobile operating system were first infected by a similar virus in August 2004. The worm, called Ojam, had engineered an anti-piracy Trojan virus in older versions of the mobile phone game Mosquito. This virus sent SMS text messages without the user's knowledge.

In June 2004, BBC reported that a handful of security companies received a proof-of-concept mobile virus, which was believed to have come from an international group of virus writers known as 29a. The worm, known as Cabir, infected phones and devices running the Symbian operating system which account for more than 80% of the GSM mobile phone market and Bluetooth wireless technology. Unsuspecting victims then thought they had received a security program and proceeded to infect themselves upon installation.

The first report of the Cabir virus in the United States was in 2005, when it infected two Nokia 6600s on display in a cell phone store in California. The source of the infection was unknown, but due to the nature of mobile devices, anyone passing the store could have passed on the virus through their built-in Bluetooth antennas. Much more harmful versions of Cabir were discovered in other countries, including Finland, where Nokia is headquartered, the U.K., and Singapore. This is thought to be by far the most damaging cell phone virus to date.

In July 2004, a proof-of-concept malicious program, Duts, demonstrated that Windows Mobile is vulnerable to infection. It attacks a pocket PC's programs and spreads each time infected programs are exchanged. When a program hit by Duts is activated, a message appears asking the user permission to proceed: *Dear User, am I allowed to spread?* If the user mistakenly grants authorization, the virus will infect all .EXE files present in the directory. Duts was created by Ratter, the pseudonym of a virus writer who is an active member of 29a.

The first appearance of Skulls, the initial version of which is called Skulls.A, dates back to November 2004. Skulls is a malicious SIS file Trojan that hides behind files named Extended Theme Manager or Timer Room. If mistakenly installed, it will cause all application icons to be replaced with a picture of a skull and cross bones. The icons will no longer refer to the actual applications, so none of the phone system applications will be able to start, other than outgoing and incoming calls. All functions needing some system application, such as SMS and MMS messaging, Web browsing, and camera, will no longer function.

In 2005, a malicious virus called "CommWarrior" began infecting Nokia Series 60 handsets running the Symbian operating system. CommWarrior uses MMS and Bluetooth wireless connections to randomly send messages with copies of itself to numbers in the infected Nokia device's address book. It can be sent to any kind of wireless gadget or computer, but if that device does not run the Symbian Series 60 software, it will not be infected. Potential targets must accept and download CommWarrior in order for the Trojan to launch itself. The virus uses more than 20 different messages to entice users to open its file, including text designed to look like legitimate software updates from Symbian or even pornographic photographs. CommWarrior differs from the Cabir virus, which was believed to be relatively harmless and used only Bluetooth to proliferate.

Later in 2005, a new virus called CARDTRP.A appeared, which attempted to be the first cross-platform mobile worm by dropping worms in the infected memory card including WUKILL.B. The virus arrives either through a Bluetooth wireless connection or by downloading it off the Web. It infects Symbian Series 60-based phones such as a number of Nokia devices, and overwrites system (sis) files with corrupted versions, causing them to malfunction. It also copies a number of other viruses to the drive E, normally associated with the memory card. Once in the memory slot of a desktop PC, the files (which include a backdoor password-stealing Trojan and a self-propagating worm) attempt to autorun.

The Redbrowser Trojan, which surfaced in 2006, was the first malware to target J2ME (Java 2 Mobile Edition) phones and represented a significant development in mobile viruses. Rather than focusing on high-end smartphones running on Symbian or Pocket PC, it works on many low-end phones with J2ME support. Redbrowser disguises itself as a WAP browser offering free WAP browsing and SMS messages in order to trick the user into sending SMS messages. In actuality, it sends numerous SMS messages to a specific number, thereby causing the user to incur charges.

Cxover is a proof-of-concept worm written in Microsoft .NET's Microsoft Intermediate Language (MSIL) that can affect both Windows desktops and Windows mobile devices with the .NET framework installed. When it infects Windows desktop PCs, the virus reproduces itself and adds a registry entry pointing to the new file so that the payload is activated each time the machine is rebooted. It then waits for an application such as ActiveSync to synchronize the Pocket PC device with the infected Windows desktop unit. When it detects a connection, it copies itself over to the mobile device. Once it is executed in the mobile environment, it deletes all files in the "My Documents" directory, copies itself to the system directory, and places a link to itself in the startup directory.

Summary

This chapter addresses issues associated with mobile payment systems. The chapter starts with a brief description of a mobile payment model that is comprised of four principal players: customer, merchant/content provider, payment service provider (PSP), and trusted third party (TTP). Then, a classification of mobile payment systems is explained. After describing the SIM-based system and the NFC-based system, the chapter closes with a discussion of security issues in terms of mobile viruses.

NOTE

1. The conversion of data into a scrambled code that can be deciphered and sent across a public or private network.

Glossary

2G

Second-Generation mobile telecommunication systems that emerged in the 1990s when mobile operators deployed the GSM and the TDMA among other standards.

3G

Third-Generation mobile telecommunication systems whose key features are built to handle the needs of high-speed Internet browsing, worldwide roaming capability, support for multimedia applications, and handheld GPS use among other data transmissions.

4G

Fourth-Generation mobile telecommunication systems that provide a comprehensive and secure all-IP-based mobile broadband solution to laptop computer wireless modems, smartphones, and other mobile devices.

A2P

Application to person.

Android

Mobile OS developed by the Open Handset Alliance led by Google.

AR

Augmented reality. A direct or indirect view of a real-world environment whose elements are augmented by computer-generated sensory input such as sound, video, graphics, or GPS data.

Biosensor

Chemical sensing device in which a biologically derived recognition entity is coupled to a transducer to allow the quantitative development of some complex biochemical parameter.

BlackBerry

Smartphone brand developed and designed by Research in Motion (RIM) since 1999.

Bluetooth

Short-range radio interface technology that provides wireless connectivity in a relatively short range.

Cloud computing

The creation of Internet-based computing infrastructure from which businesses and users are able to access applications from anywhere on demand.

CRM

Customer Relationship Management. Methodology and tools used to enhance interactions between an organization and its clients.

Cryptography

The science of rendering information unintelligible to all but its senders and receivers.

Customer loyalty programs

Programs sponsored by a firm to encourage customer repeat purchases through program enrollment processes and the distribution of awards, discount coupons, etc.

Diffusion of innovations theory

A theory proposed by Everett Rogers in 1962 that posits that diffusion is the process by which an innovation is communicated through certain channels over time among the members of a social system.

EDM

Expectation-Disconfirmation model that posits that expectations (what was expected), coupled with expectancy disconfirmation (what was observed), lead to post-purchase satisfaction.

FeliCa

Contactless RFID smart card system from Sony in Japan, primarily used in *Osaifu Ketai*, a mobile wallet system that stores electronic money cards in mobile phones.

Galapagos effect

Refers to the Japanese super-powerful mobile ecosystem with futuristic technologies, business models, and experiences that was carefully incubated in isolation and so unique it would evolve apart from outside influence.

GIS

Geographic Information System. A system designed to capture, store, manipulate, analyze, manage, and present geographical data.

Google Wallet

Mobile payment system developed by Google that allows users to store credit cards, loyalty cards, and gift cards, among other things, as well as to redeem sales promotions on their mobile phones.

GPS

Global Positioning System. A system that provides specially coded satellite signals that can be processed in a GPS receiver, enabling the receiver to compute position, velocity, and time. Funded by and controlled by the U.S. Department of Defense.

GSM

Global System for Mobile Communication. The world's most widely used 2G mobile communication system, first launched in Finland in 1991.

Hz

Hertz. A radio frequency measurement in which one hertz equals one cycle per second.

i-mode

NTT DoCoMo's mobile Internet service and its portal with packet network and server system.

Intra-BAN communication
Communication between the nodes and the MBU.

iOS
Apple's mobile OS. Formerly known as iPhone OS.

IP
Internet Protocol.

iPhone
Apple's smartphone brand. The first iPhone was unveiled by Apple's former CEO Steve Jobs on January 9, 2007, and released on June 29, 2007.

IS
Information System.

LBS
Location-based services that provided users with geographically oriented data and information services across mobile telecommunication networks.

LTE
Long Term Evolution is a standard for wireless communication of high-speed data.

Mbps
Megabits per second.

Microsoft Tags
Unique two-dimensional color codes that can be used to open URLs or multimedia files.

MMS
Multimedia Message Service.

Mobile commerce (m-commerce)
The one- or two-way exchange of value facilitated by a mobile consumer electronic device (e.g., mobile handset) that is enabled by wireless technologies and communication networks.

Mobile Marketing

A set of practices that enables organizations to communicate and engage with their audience in an interactive and relevant manner through any mobile device or network.

Motivations

The type of perceived incentives or rewards that can drive an individual to choose and engage in media use.

NFC

Near field communication. A system that allows a mobile device to collect data from another device or NFC tag in close proximity.

Opt-in

Process of actively granting permission to send a user a promotional message or to collect personal information for marketing purposes.

Opt-out

Process of giving a user the choice to receive or not any promotional message or to have his or her personal information collected for marketing purposes.

OS

Operating system.

Packet

A small unit of data routed through a network based on the destination address contained within each packet.

Pull mobile advertising

Any promotional message sent to a mobile subscriber upon request or placed on browsed wireless content.

Push mobile advertising

Any promotional message sent to a mobile device without a prior request.

QR code

Quick Response code. A two-dimensional bar code consisting of black modules arranged in a square pattern on a white background. Developed by Denso Wave in 1994.

RFID
Radio frequency identification. A system that transmits the identity (in the form of a unique serial number) of an object or person wirelessly, using radio waves.

Situation awareness
Perception of the elements of the environment within a volume of time and space, the comprehension of their meaning and the projection of their status in the near future.

SMS
Short Message Service. A service for sending messages up to 160 characters long to mobile phones.

SNS
Social Networking Site.

TAM
Technology Acceptance Model. An extension of TRA that more specifically focuses on the prediction of the acceptability of an IS. The TAM suggests that the acceptability of an IS is determined by two main factors: perceived usefulness and perceived ease of use.

TDMA
Time Division Multiple Access. A technology used in 2G mobile communication systems.

Time-geography
An academic discipline that attempts to examine the coordination of individuals' possibilities of action in time and space in terms of three types of constraints: capability, coupling, and authority.

TPB
Theory of Planned Behavior. An extension of the TRA that attempts to overcome the original model's limitations in dealing with behaviors over which people have incomplete volitional control.

TRA
Theory of Reasoned Action, developed by Martin Fishbein and Icek Ajzen in

1975 to examine the relationship between attitudes and behavior. TRA looks at behavioral intentions rather than attitudes as the main predictors of behavior.

Ubiquity
Flexibility of time and location that can be further decomposed into immediacy, continuity, portability, and searchability, among other dimensions.

UMTS
Universal Mobile Telecommunication Service. A3G broadband, packet-based transmission of text, digitized voice, video, and multimedia at data rates up to 2 Mbps.

UPC
Universal Product Code.

UTAUT
Unified Theory of Acceptance and Use of Technology that aims to explain user intentions to use an IS and subsequent usage behavior. The theory holds that four key constructs (performance expectancy, effort expectancy, social influence, and facilitating conditions) are direct determinants of usage intention and behavior.

WAP
Wireless Application Protocol. An open global specification that enables mobile users with wireless devices to access and interact with information and services.

Wayfinding
A consistent use and organization of definite sensory cues from the external environment.

WBSN
Wearable Body Sensor Network. A system formed with the wearable or implantable biosensors in a patient's body.

WLAN
Wireless Local Area Network. A network linking two or more computers without wires (cables).

References

2D Barcode Strategy. (2011, January 11). JetBlue uses QR code. http://www.2d-barcodestrategy.com/2011/01/jetblue-uses-qr-code.html, accessed on August 25, 2011.

2D Code. (2011a, September 12). Sony Music QR code ads in London cabs. Asides. http://2d-code.co.uk/qr-code-ads-in-london-cabs/, accessed on September 15, 2011.

2D Code. (2011b, September 21). Halloween cards get a QR code. http://2d-code.co.uk/halloween-card-qr-code/, accessed on September 15, 2011.

3GVision. (2011, August 3). Global growth in mobile barcode usage—Q2/2011. 3GVision News. http://www.i-nigma.com/pr27.html, accessed on October 14, 2011.

4G Americas (2011). Understanding 1G vs. 2G vs. 3G vs. 4G. Technology Center. http://www.4gamericas.org/index.cfm?fuseaction=page&sectionid=361, accessed on August 2, 2011.

ABC News. (2011, April 22). Why are Apple, Google tracking your phone? http://abcnews.go.com/Technology/google-apple-track-users-location-information/story?id=13436330, accessed on June 3, 2011.

About.com. (2011, June 6). What are iPad sales to date? iPhone/iPod. http://ipod.about.com/od/ipad-modelsandterms/f/ipad-sales-to-date.htm, accessed on August 22, 2011.

Adams, P.C. (1995). A reconsideration of personal boundaries in space-time. *Annals of the Association of American Geographers, 85*(2), 267–285.

Ajzen, I. (1991). The theory of planned behavior. *Organizational Behavior and Human Decision Processes, 50*(2), 179–211.

Ajzen, I., & Fishbein, M. (1980). *Understanding attitudes and predicting social behavior.* Upper Saddle River, NJ: Prentice-Hall.

Ajzen, I., Nichols, A.J., & Driver, B.L. (1995). Identifying salient beliefs about leisure activities: Frequency of elicitation versus response latency. *Journal of Applied Social Psychology, 25*(16), 1391–1410.

Alfaro, I., Nardon, M., Pianesi, P., Stock, O., & Zancanaro, M. (2004). Using cinematic techniques on mobile devices for cultural tourism. *Information Technology & Tourism, 7*(2), 223–230.

All Facebook. (2010, August 24). Coca-Cola marketing event tracked Facebook users via RFID. http://www.allfacebook.com/coca-cola-marketing-2010–08, accessed on August 2, 2011.

Allen, G.L. (1999). Spatial abilities, cognitive maps, and wayfinding: Bases for individual differences in spatial cognition and behavior. In R.G. Golledge (Ed.), *Wayfinding behavior: Cognitive mapping and other spatial processes* (pp. 46–80). Baltimore: The Johns Hopkins University Press.

Amazon.com. (2011). Kindle Keyboard 3G. http://www.amazon.com/Kindle-Wireless-Reader-3G-Wifi-Graphite/dp/B002FQJT3Q, accessed on October 11, 2011.

Anderson, E.W., & Sullivan, M.W. (1993). The antecedents and consequences of customer satisfaction for firms. *Marketing Science, 12*(2), 125–143.

Android Community. (2011, June 29). Google Android market reaches 4.5 billion downloads. http://androidcommunity.com/google-android-market-reaches-4–5-billion-downloads-20110629/, accessed on September 2, 2011.

Apple. (2011a). HTML5 and Web standards. HTML5. http://www.apple.com/html5/, accessed on October 22, 2011.

Apple. (2011b, July 7). Apple's App store downloads top 15 billion. Apple Press Info, http://www.apple.com/pr/library/2011/07/07Apples-App-Store-Downloads-Top-15-Billion.html, accessed on July 22, 2011.

Apple. (2011c). iPad: Technical specifications. http://www.apple.com/ipad/specs/, accessed on July 23, 2011.

Armstrong, G.B., & Sopory, P. (1997). Effects of background television on phonological and visuospatial working memory. *Communication Research, 24*(5), 459–480.

Aware Home Research Initiative. (2010). http://awarehome.imtc.gatech.edu/, Georgia Institute of Technology.

Balasubramanian, S., Peterson, R.A., & Jarvenpaa, S.L. (2002). Exploring the implications of m-commerce for markets and marketing. *Journal of the Academy of Marketing Science, 30*(4), 348–361.

Baldi, S., & Thaung, P.P. (2002). The entertaining way to M-commerce: Japan's approach to the mobile Internet—A model for Europe? *Electronic Markets, 12*(1), 6–13.

Bandura, A. (1982). Self-efficacy mechanism in human agency. *American Psychologist, 37*(2), 122–147.

Barnes, S.J. (2002). Wireless digital advertising: Nature and implications. *International Journal of Advertising, 21*(3), 399–420.

Barnes, S.J., & Huff, S.L. (2003). Rising sun: iMode and the wireless Internet. *Communication of the ACM, 46*(11), 79–84.

Baron, N.S. (2008). Adjusting the volume: Technology and multitasking in discourse control. In J.E. Katz (Ed.), *Handbook of mobile communication studies* (pp. 177–193). Cambridge, MA: MIT Press.

Barwise, P., & Strong, C. (2002). Permission-based mobile advertising. *Journal of Interactive Marketing, 16*(1), 14–24.

Beach, L.R., & Mitchell, T.R. (1998). The basics of image theory. In L.R. Beach (Ed.), *Image theory: Theoretical and empirical foundations* (pp. 3–18). Mahwah, NJ: Lawrence Erlbaum Associates.

Belk, R.W. (1975). Situational variables and consumer behavior. *Journal of Consumer Research, 2*(3), 157–164.

Berry, L.L., Seiders, K., & Grewal, D. (2002, July). Understanding service convenience. *Journal of Marketing, 66*, 1–17.

Bhattacherjee, A. (2001). Understanding information systems continuance: An expectation-confirmation model. *MIS Quarterly*, *25*(3), 351–370.

BIA/Kelsey. (2011, June 23). U.S. mobile local ad revenues to grow from $404 million in 2010 to $2.8 billion in 2015, according to BIA/Kelsey. Press Release. http://www.biakelsey.com/Company/Press-Releases/110623-U.S.-Mobile-Local-Ad-Revenues-to-Grow-from-$404-Million-in-2010-to-$2.8-Billion-in-2015.asp, accessed on August 23, 2011.

Blackwell, R.D., Miniard, P.W., & Engel, J.F. (2006). *Consumer behavior* (10th ed.). Mason, OH: Thomson Higher Education.

Bluetooth. (2010). Basics. http://www.bluetooth.com/English/Technology/Pages/Basics.aspx#5, accessed on September 22, 2011.

Bombara, M., Cali, D., & Santoro, C. (2003). KORE: A multi-agent system to assist museum visitor. In G. Armano, F. De Paoli, A. Omicini, & E. Vargiu (Eds.), *Proceedings of the Joint Workshop "From Objects to Agents": Intelligent systems and pervasive computing (WOA2003)* (pp. 175–178). Milan, Italy: Pitagora Editrice Bologna.

Brimicombe, A., & Li, Y. (2006). Mobile space-time envelopes for location-based services. *Transactions in GIS*, *10*(1), 5–23.

Brombach, B., Bruns, E., & Bimber, O. (2009). Subobject detection through spatial relationships on mobile phones. In B. Brombach, E. Bruns, & O. Bimber (Eds.), *Proceedings of International Conference of Intelligent User Interfaces (IUI2009)* (pp. 267–276). New York: ACM Press.

Bruner, G.C., & Kumar, A. (2005). Explaining consumer acceptance of handheld Internet devices. *Journal of Business Research*, *58*, 553–558.

Bruns, E., & Bimber, O. (2008a). Adaptive training of video sets for image recognition on mobile phones. *Personal and Ubiquitous Computing*, *13*(2), 165–178.

Bruns, E., & Bimber, O. (2008b). Phone-to-phone communication for adaptive image classification. In G. Kotsis, D. Taniar, E. Pardede, & I. Khalil (Eds.), *Proceedings of International Conference on Advances in Mobile Computing & Multimedia (MoMM2008)* (pp. 276–281). New York: ACM Press.

Bruns, E., & Bimber, O. (2010a). Localization and classification through adaptive pathway analysis. *IEEE Pervasive Computing*, *99*(1), 1–7.

Bruns, E., & Bimber, O. (2010b). Mobile museum guidance using relational multi-image classification. In R. Klamma, H. Kosch, M. Lux, & F. Stegmaier (Eds.), *Proceedings of International Conference on Multimedia and Ubiquitous Engineering (MUE2010)* (pp. 1–8). Tilburg, The Netherlands: CEUR-WS.

Bruns, E., Brombach, B., & Bimber, O. (2008). Mobile phone enabled museum guidance with adaptive classification. *IEEE Computer Graphics and Applications*, *28*(4), 98–102.

Bruns, E., Brombach, B., Zeidler, T., & Bimber, O. (2007). Enabling mobile phones to support large-scale museum guidance. *IEEE Multimedia*, *14*(2), 16–25.

Business Insider. (2011, March 31). Google kills off those little square codes you scan with your phone. http://www.businessinsider.com/those-little-square-codes-you-scan-with-your-phone-are-dead-2011-3#ixzz1Z3LmKt7b, accessed on July 21, 2011.

Butcher, D. (2009, July 2). Unilever's Rexona runs "Detective Stripes" mobile ad campaign. Mobile Marketing. http://www.mobilemarketer.com/cms/news/advertising/3597.print, accessed on September 25, 2010.

Carden, N. (2007, May). iTunes and iPod in the Enterprise. *ISSA Journal*, 22–25.

Chassin, L., Presson, C.C., Sherman, S.J., & Edwards, D.A. (1991). Four pathways to young-adult smoking status: Adolescent social-psychological antecedents in a Midwestern community sample. *Health Psychology, 10*(6), 409–418.

Chen, J., & Ringel, M. (2001). Can advergaming be the future of interactive advertising? The kpe Fast Forward white paper series. Requested by email (fastforward@kpe.com).

Chen, J.V., Ross, W., & Huang, S.F. (2004). Privacy, trust, and justice considerations for location-based mobile telecommunication services. *Info, 10*(4), 30–45.

Choi, Y.K., Hwang, J.S., & McMillan, S.J. (2008). Gearing up for mobile advertising: A cross-cultural examination of key factors that drive mobile messages home to consumers. *Psychology & Marketing, 25*(8), 756–768.

Cialdini, R.B., Kallgren, C.A., & Reno, R.R. (1991). A focus theory of normative conduct. *Advances in Experimental Social Psychology, 24*, 201–234.

Cloud Computing World. (2011). Ten ways Cloud Computing can help your business. Cloud Computing for Businesses. http://www.cloudcomputingworld.org/cloud-computing-for-businesses/ten-ways-cloud-computing-can-help-your-business.html, accessed on October 3, 2011.

Cloud Tweaks. (2011, April 26). Cloud Computing market will top $241 billion in 2020. The Network Architect's Almanac, http://www.cloudtweaks.com/2011/04/cloud-computing-market-will-top-241-billion-in-2020/, accessed on May 23, 2011.

CNET. (2011, January 18). IDC: Apple iPad secures 87 percent market share. The Digital Home. http://news.cnet.com/8301–13506_3–20028801–17.html#ixzz1ZS3yQ7LP, accessed on March 2, 2011.

Computerworld. (2011, July 26). App Store, Android Market spur explosive app download growth: Researcher In-Stat projects 48 billion app downloads by 2015 generating more than $29 billion in app revenue. News. http://www.computerworld.com/s/article/9218654/App_Store_Android_Market_spur_explosive_app_download_growth, accessed on July 28, 2011.

comScore. (2008, October 31). SMS advertising for non-mobile products grows as mobile is integrated into marketing budgets for consumer goods and services. Press Release. http://www.comscore.com/Press_Events/Press_Releases/2008/10/SMS_Advertising_Grows, accessed on June 2, 2010.

comScore. (2011). Mobile 2010 year review. http://www.comscore.com/Press_Events/Presentations_Whitepapers/2011/2010_Mobile_Year_in_Review, accessed on September 5, 2011.

Condayan, C. (2010). mHealth: Infectious disease in a mobile age. DnaTube. http://www.dnatube.com/video/3873/mHealth-Infectious-Disease-in-a-Mobile-Age#addfavour, accessed on May 2, 2011.

Coors, V., Elting, C., Kray, C., & Laakso, K. (2005). Presenting route instructions on mobile devices: From textual directions to 3D visualization. In J. Dykes, A.M. MacEachren, & M.-J. Kraak (Eds.), *Exploring geovisualization* (pp. 529–550). Amsterdam: Elsevier.

Cross-marketing. (2010). A survey on consumers' usage of coupon and net money. http://www.cross-m.co.jp/report/report.html$/id/184/, accessed on March 22, 2011 (in Japanese).

Culture24. (2009, April 21). Yorkshire Dales go hi-tech with Bluetooth guided tours. http://www.culture24.0rg.uk/science+%26+nature/technology/art67800, accessed on September 2, 2010.

Cyr, D., Head, M., & Ivanov, A. (2006). Design aesthetics leading to m-loyalty in mobile commerce. *Information & Management, 43*(8), 950–963.

Dahlberg, T., Mallat, N., Ondrus, J., & Zmijewska, A. (2008). Past, present and future of mobile payment research: A literature review. *Electronic Commerce Research and Applications, 7*, 165–181.

Dao, D., Rizos, C., & Wang, J.L. (2002). Location-based services: Technical and business issues. *GPS Solutions, 6*, 169–178.

Davis, F.D. (1986). *A technology acceptance model for empirically testing new end-user information systems: Theory and results.* Unpublished doctoral dissertation, Sloan School of Management, Massachusetts Institute of Technology.

Davis, F.D. (1989). Perceived usefulness, perceived ease of use, and user acceptance of information technology. *MIS Quarterly, 13*(3), 319–339.

Davis, F.D., Bagozzi, R.P., & Warshaw, P.R. (1989). User acceptance of computer technology: A comparison of two theoretical models. *Management Science, 35*(8), 982–1003.

Davis, R., & Sajtos, L. (2008). Measuring consumer interactivity in response to campaigns coupling mobile and television media. *Journal of Advertising Research, 48*(3), 375–391.

DBIS (Discoveries and Breakthroughs Inside Science). (2010). Tracking travelers at the airport civil engineers design Bluetooth system to monitor airport security line wait time. http://www.aip.org/dbis/stories/2010/20029.html, accessed on March 1, 2011.

Denso Wave. (2010). QR code features. QR Code.com. http://www.denso-wave.com/qrcode/qrfeature-e.html, accessed on September 22, 2011.

Desai, M., Louer, G., King, R., & Wolvin, M. (2011). LBS marketing—Why the federal government cares and what you can do about it. MMA. http://mmaglobal.com/files/MMA_Desai_Mobile_Marketing_Article%209-27-11_WP.pdf, accessed on October 2, 2011.

Dexigner. (2010, November 13). GoldRun builds first invisible pop-up store for Airwalk. http://www.dexigner.com/news/21856.

Dickinger, A., & Kleijnen, M. (2008). Coupons going wireless: Determinants of consumer intentions to redeem mobile coupons. *Journal of Interactive Marketing, 22*(3), 23–39.

Digital Transactions. (2011, September 11). Google announces commercial launch of its much-anticipated NFC Mobile Wallet. News. http://www.digitaltransactions.net/news/story/3210, accessed on September 22, 2011.

Dillemuth, J. (2005). Map design evaluation for mobile display. *Cartography and Geographic Information Science, 32*, 285–301.

The Drum. (2011, May 21). Cloud computing: Hidden danger to everyone's civil liberties? News. http://www.thedrum.co.uk/news/2011/05/21/21751-cloud-computing-hidden-danger-to-everyone-s-civil-liberties-exclusive/, accessed on September 2, 2011.

eMarketer. (2008). *Mobile location-based services.* New York: eMarketer.

eMarketer. (2011, January 12). Facebook drives US social network ad spending past $3 billion in 2011. http://www.emarketer.com/Article.aspx?R=1008180, accessed on July 16, 2011.

Endsley, M.R. (1988). Design and evaluation for situation awareness enhancement. In *Proceedings of the Human Factors and Ergonomics Society 32nd Annual Meeting* (pp. 97–102), Santa Monica, CA: Human Factors and Ergonomics Society.

Evans, J.A., & Sterry P. (1999). Portable computers and interactive multimedia: A new paradigm for interpreting museum collections. In D. Bearman & J. Trant (Eds.), *Cultural heritage informatics 1999: Selected papers from ICHIM99* (pp. 113–126). Pittsburgh: Archives & Museum Informatics.

Featherman, M.S., & Pavlou, P.A. (2003). Predicting e-services adoption: A perceived risk perspective. *International Journal of Human-Computer Studies, 59*, 451–474.

Ferris, M. (2007). Insights on mobile advertising, promotion, and research. *Journal of Advertising Research, 47*(1), 28–37.

FierceDeveloper. (2011, January 22). Ten billion downloads and counting: The history of Apple's App Store, and its all-time top apps. http://www.fiercedeveloper.com/special-reports/ten-billion-downloads-and-counting-history-apples-app-store-and-its-all-tim#ixzz1bDQVUyAK, accessed on September 22, 2011.

FierceMobileContent. (2011, August 18). SMS: The dying cash cow for wireless carriers? http://www.fiercemobilecontent.com/print/node/19711, accessed on September 30, 2011.

First Company. (2011, August 19). Wherever you go, Yelp Mobile and its 20 million reviews and deals will find you. http://www.fastcompany.com/1774494/colocation-with-howard-lindzon-yelp-in-san-francisco-ca, accessed on August 31, 2011.

Fishbein, M., & Ajzen, I. (1975). *Belief, attitude, intention and behavior: An introduction to theory and research*. Reading, MA: Addison-Wesley.

Föckler, P., Zeidler, T., Brombach, B., Bruns, E., & Bimber, O. (2005). PhoneGuide: Museum guidance supported by on-device object recognition on mobile phones. In M. Billinghurst (Ed.), *Proceedings of International Conference on Mobile and Ubiquitous Computing (MUM2005)* (pp. 3–10). New York: ACM Press.

Gao, Q., Rau, P., & Salvendy, G. (2009). Perception of interactivity: Affects of four key variables in mobile advertising. *International Journal of Human-Computer Interaction, 25*(6), 479–505.

Gartner. (2011, June 16). Gartner says worldwide mobile advertising revenue forecast to reach $3.3 billion in 2011. Press Release. http://www.gartner.com/it/page.jsp?id=1726614, accessed on September 5, 2011.

Geelan, J. (2009, January 24). Twenty-one experts define cloud computing: It is the infrastructural paradigm shift that is sweeping across the Enterprise IT world, but how is it best defined? *Cloud Computing Journal*, http://cloudcomputing.sys-con.com/node/612375, accessed on September 15, 2011.

Gibbs, M. (2007, November 29). Virtualization mojo. Network World. http://www.networkworld.com/community/toolshed/mark-gibbs/virtualization-mojo, accessed on July 27, 2011.

Godin, G., & Kok, G. (1996). The theory of planned behavior: A review of its applications in health-related behaviors. *American Journal of Health Promotion, 11*, 87–98.

Gogan, J.L., Williams, C.B., & Fedorowicz, J. (2007). RFID and interorganisational collaboration: Political and administrative challenges. *Electronic Government, an International Journal, 4*(4) 423–435.

Golembiewski, R.T., & McConkie, M. (1975). The centrality of interpersonal trust in group processes. In C.L. Cooper (Ed.), *Theories of group processes* (pp. 131–185). New York: John Wiley & Sons.

Golledge, R.G. (Ed.). (1999). *Wayfinding behavior: Cognitive mapping and other spatial processes*. Baltimore: The Johns Hopkins University Press.

Golledge, R.G., & Stimson, R.J. (1997). *Spatial behaviour: A geographical perspective*. New York: Guilford Press.

Google. (2009, December 7). Explore a whole new way to window shop, with Google and your mobile phone. The Official Google Blog. http://googleblog.blogspot.com/2009/12/explore-whole-new-way-to-window-shop.html, accessed on March 2, 2010.

Google. (2011). Using gmail, calendar and docs without an Internet connection. Google Enterprise Blog. August 31. http://googleenterprise.blogspot.com/2011/08/using-gmail-calendar-and-docs-without.html, accessed on September 3, 2011.

Goren-Bar, D., Graziola, I., Kuflik, T., Pianesi, F., Rocchi, C., Stock, O., & Zancanaro, M. (2005). I like it–An affective interface for a multimodal museum guide. In *Proceedings of Intelligent User Interfaces IUI'05*, San Diego, CA. http://peach.itc.it/papers/gorenbar2005.pdf., accessed on January 20, 2006.

Ha, I., Yoon, Y., & Choi, M. (2007). Determinants of adoption of mobile games under mobile broadband wireless access environment. *Information & Management, 44*, 276–286.

Hägerstrand, T. (1965). Quantitative techniques for the analysis of the spread of information and technology. In C.A. Anderson & M.J. Bowman (Eds.), *Education and economic development* (pp. 244–280). Chicago: Aldine Publishers.

Hägerstrand, T. (1967). *Innovation diffusion as a spatial process.* Chicago: University of Chicago Press.

Hägerstrand, T. (1970). What about people in regional science? *Papers of the Regional Science Association, 24*, 7–21.

Hägerstrand, T. (1975). Space, time and human conditions. In A. Karlqvist, L. Lundquist, & F. Snickars (Eds.), *Dynamic allocation of urban space* (pp. 3–14). Farnborough, UK: Saxon House.

Hanson, M.A., Powell, H.C., & Barth, A.T. (2009). Body area sensor networks: Challenges and opportunities. *Computer, 42*, 58–65.

Hassinen, M., Hyppönen, K., & Trichina, E. (2007). Utilizing national public-key infrastructure in mobile payment systems. *Electronic Commerce Research and Applications, 7*, 214–231.

Hennig-Thurau, T., Gwinner, K.P., Walsh, G., & Gremler, D.D. (2004). Electronic word-of-mouth via consumer-opinion platforms: What motivates consumers to articulate themselves on the Internet? *Journal of Interactive Marketing, 18*(1), 38–52.

Hertel, G., Aarts, H., & Zeelenberg, M. (2002). What do you think is "fair"? Effects of ingroup norms and outcome control on fairness judgments. *European Journal of Social Psychology, 32*, 327–341.

Hoffman, D.L., Novak, T.P., & Venkatesh, A. (2004). Has the Internet become indispensable? *Communications of the ACM, 47*(7), 37–42.

Höflich J.R., & Rössler, P. (2001). Mobile schriftliche Kommunikation oder: EMail für das andy. *Medien & Kommunikationswissenschaft, 49*, 437–461.

Holbrook, M.B., & Lehmann, D.R. (1981, March). Patterns of allocating discretionary times: Complementarity among activities. *Journal of Consumer Research, 7*, 395–406.

Hong, S.J., Thong, J.Y.L., & Tam, K.Y. (2006). Understanding continued information technology usage behavior: A comparison of three models in the context of mobile Internet. *Decision Support System, 42*, 1819–1834.

Hoyer, W.D., & MacInnis, D.J. (2001). *Consumer behavior* (2nd ed.). New York: Houghton Mifflin Company.

Hsu, C.L., & Lu, H.P. (2004). Why do people play on-line games? An extended TAM with social influences and flow experience. *Information & Management, 41*(7), 853–868.

Hsu, C.L., Lu, H.P., & Hsu, H.H. (2007). Adoption of the mobile Internet: An empirical study of multimedia message service (MMS). *Omega, 35*, 715–726.

Hung, S.Y., Ku, C.K., & Chang, C.M. (2003), Critical factors of WAP services adoption: An empirical study. *Electronic Commerce Research and Application, 2*(1), 42–60.

Husson, T. (2011, May 3). Why the "web versus application" debate is irrelevant. Marketing & Strategy. Forrester Blogs. http://blogs.forrester.com/thomas_husson/11–05–03-why_the_web_versus_application_debate_is_irrelevant, accessed on July 23, 2011.

impress R&D (2007). *Ketai Hakusyo*, impress R&D, Mobile Content Forum, and Access Media (Eds.). Tokyo: impress R&D (in Japanese).

The Independent. (2010, August 23). How to use Facebook Places while protecting your private information. Gadgets & Tech. http://www.independent.co.uk/life-style/gadgets-and-tech/how-to-use-facebook-places-while-protecting-your-private-information-2059813.html, accessed on October 2, 2011.

InfoWorld. (2011, July 21). Will HTML5 kill the mobile app? With a powerful new upgrade to HTML now emerging, developers may opt for apps that run in mobile browsers. Java World. http://www.javaworld.com/javaworld/jw-07–2011/110720-will-html5-kill-mobile-apps.html?page=2, accessed on September 15, 2011.

International Business Times. (2011, March 31). Google kills QR codes in favor of NFC. http://www.ibtimes.com/articles/129307/20110331/google-qr-codes-nfc-google-places.htm, accessed on August 3, 2011.

Internet Retailer. (2011a, June 22). One-fourth of iPhone owners and one-fifth of Android owners use m-commerce apps. Technology. http://www.internetretailer.com/2011/06/22/one-fourth-iphone-and-android-owners-use-m-commerce-apps, accessed on September 2, 2011.

Internet Retailer. (2011b, August 2). 33 million consumers shop with a mobile phone. Technology. http://www.internetretailer.com/2011/08/02/33-million-consumers-shop-mobile-phone, accessed on August 22, 2011.

iShare. (2009, March 6). One fourth register in coupon service at fast-food restaurants. First-food coupon usage survey (2nd). http://release.center.jp/2009/03/0601.html, accessed on July 2, 2011.

ITU. (2010). The world in 2010: Facts and figures. http://www.itu.int/ITU-D/ict/material/FactsFigures2010.pdf, accessed on September 22, 2011.

Jacoby, J., Szybillo, G.J., & Berning, C.K. (1976, March). Time and consumer behavior: An interdisciplinary overview. *Journal of Consumer Research, 2*, 320–339.

Janelle, D.G. (1973). Measuring human extensibility in a shrinking world. *Journal of Geography, 72*(5), 5–10.

Janelle, D.G. (2004). Impact of information technologies. In S. Hanson & G. Giuliano (Eds.), *The geography of urban transportation* (3rd ed., pp. 86–112). New York: Guilford.

Jansen, W., & Scarfone, K. (2008). *Guidelines on cell phone and PDA security: Recommendations of the National Institute of Standards and Technology.* NIST Special Publication 800–124, National Institute of Standards and Technology, Washington D.C.: US Department of Commerce.

Jayawardhena, C., Kuckertz, A., Karjaluoto, H., & Kautonen, T. (2009). Antecedents to permission based mobile marketing: An initial examination. *European Journal of Marketing, 43*(3/4), 473–499.

Jiang, B., & Yao, X. (2006). Location-based services and GIS in perspective. *Computers, Environment and Urban Systems, 30*(6), 712–725.

Jones, D., Bellomo, R., Bates, S., Warrillow, S., Goldsmith, D., Hart, G., & Opdam, H. (2006). Patient monitoring and the timing of cardiac arrests and medical emergency team calls in a teaching hospital. *Intensive Care Medicine, 32*, 1352–1356.

Juniper Research (2011). "Press Release: eReader Shipments to Reach 67m by 2016, Up from 25m in 2011, Despite Tablet Threat," November 15. http://juniperresearch.com/viewpressrelease.php?pr=272. accessed on April 3, 2012.

Juniper Research. (2011, May 4). Application generated mobile texts to exceed $70 billion revenues by 2016, overtaking person-to-person messaging, says Juniper Research. Press Release. http://www.juniperresearch.com/viewpressrelease.php?pr=242, accessed on May 30, 2011.

Karim, W. (2004). The privacy implications of personal locators: Why you should think twice before voluntarily availing yourself to GPS monitoring. *Journal of Law & Policy, 14*, 485–515.

Kato, H., Tan, T.K., & Chai, D. (2010). *Barcodes for mobile devices.* Cambridge: Cambridge University Press.

Kats, R. (2011a, May 26). Twentieth Century Fox taps NFC-enabled posters for mobile film campaign. Mobile Marketer. http://www.mobilemarketer.com/cms/news/advertising/10029.html, accessed on January 6, 2012.

Kats, R. (2011b, August 3). McDonald's taps augmented reality, mobile check-ins for Smurfs promotion. Mobile Commerce Daily. http://www.mobilecommercedaily.com/2011/08/03/mcdonald%E2%80%99s-taps-augmented-reality-mobile-check-ins-for-smurfs-promotion, accessed on August 11, 2011.

Katz, E., Blumler, J.G., & Gurevitch, M. (1974). Utilization of mass communication by the individuals. In J.G. Blumler & E. Katz (Eds.), *The uses of mass communication* (pp. 19–32). Beverly Hills, CA: Sage.

Kelley, E.J. (1958). The importance of convenience in consumer purchasing. *Journal of Marketing, 23*(1), 32–38.

Kenyon, S. (2008). Internet use and time use—The importance of multitasking. *Time & Society, 17*(2), 283–318.

Kenyon, S., & Lyons, G. (2007). Introducing multitasking to the study of travel and ICT: examining its extent and assessing its potential importance. *Transportation Research, 41*(A), 161–175.

Kerlinger, F.N. (1979). *Behavioral research: A conceptual approach.* New York: Holt, Rinehart and Winston.

Khan, P., Hussain, A., & Kwak, K.S. (2009). Medical applications of wireless body area networks. *International Journal of Digital Content Technology and Its Applications, 3*(3), 185–193.

Khan, R., & Kellner, D. (2004). New media and Internet activism: from the "Battle of Seattle" to blogging. *New Media & Society, 6*(1): 87–95.

Kim, G.S., Park, S.B., & Oh, J.S. (2008). An examination of factors influencing consumer adoption of short message service (SMS). *Psychology & Marketing, 25*(8), 769–786.

Kleijnen, M., de Ruyter, K., & Wetzels, M. (2007). An assessment of value creation in mobile service delivery and the moderating role of time consciousness. *Journal of Retailing, 83*(1), 33–46.

Ko, E., Kim, E.Y., & Lee, E.K. (2008). Modeling consumer adoption of mobile shopping for fashion products in Korea. *Psychology and Marketing, 26*, 669–687.

Kobayashi, M. (2010). *Mobile computing: The future iPhone and Android are aiming at.* Tokyo: PHP Research Institute (in Japanese).

Korhonen, I., Pärkkä, J., & van Gils, M. (2003). Health monitoring in the home of the future. *IEEE Engineering in Medicine and Biology Magazine, 22*(3), 66–73.

Langlotz, T., & Bimber, O. (2007). Unsynchronized 4D barcodes. In *Proceedings of International Symposium on Visual Computing (ISVC2007)* (pp. 363–374). Berlin: Springer-Verlag.

Lederer, A.L., Maupin, D.L., Sena, M.P., & Zhuang, Y. (2000). The technology acceptance model and the World Wide Web. *Decision Support System, 29*, 269–282.

Leek, S., & Christodoulides, G. (2009). Next-generation mobile marketing: How young consumers react to Bluetooth-enabled advertising. *Journal of Advertising Research, 49*(1), 44–53.

Legris, P., Ingham, J., & Collerette, P. (2003). Why do people use information technology? A critical review of the technology acceptance model. *Information & Management, 40*, 191–204.

Lenntorp, B. (1999). Time-geography—at the end of its beginning. *GeoJournal, 48*, 155–158.

Leung, L., & Wei, R. (2000). More than just talk on the move: Uses and gratifications of the cellular phone. *Journalism and Mass Communication Quarterly, 77*(2), 308–320.

Li, H., & Dou, X. (2008). Creative use of QR codes in consumer communication. *International Journal of Mobile Marketing, 3*(2), 61–67.

Lifehacker. (2009, July 29). The hidden risks of cloud computing. Top News. http://lifehacker.com /5325169/the-hidden-risks-of-cloud-computing, accessed on September 12, 2011.

Lightspeed Research. (2010, October 11). 29% of European mobile consumers respond to mobile adverts they see. http://www.lightspeedresearch.com/press-releases/29-of-european-mobile-consumers-respond-to-mobile-adverts-they-see/, accessed on September 30, 2011.

Lin, C.A. (1999). Uses and gratifications. In G. Stone, M. Singletary, & V.P. Richmond (Eds.), *Clarifying communication theories: A hands-on approach* (pp. 199–208). Ames: Iowa State University Press.

Litvin, S.W., Goldsmith, R.E., & Pan, B. (2008). Electronic word-of-mouth in hospitality and tourism management. *Tourism Management, 29*(3), 458–468.

Liu, T.C., Wang, H.Y., Liang, J.K., Chan, T.W., Ko, H.W., & Yang, J.C. (2003). Wireless and mobile technologies to enhance teaching and learning. *Journal of Computer Assisted Learning, 19*, 371–382.

Lu, J., Liu, C., & Yao, J.E. (2003). Technology acceptance model for wireless Internet. *Internet Research: Electronic Networking Applications and Policy, 13*(3), 206–222.

Lu, J., Yao, J.E., & Yu, C.S. (2005). Personal innovativeness, social influences and adoption of wireless Internet services via mobile technology. *The Journal of Strategic Information Systems, 14*(3), 245–268.

Luarn, P., & Lin, H.H. (2005). Toward an understanding of the behavioral intention to use mobile banking. *Computers in Human Behavior, 21*(6), 873–891.

Lundblud, J.P. (2003). A review and critique of Rogers' diffusion of innovation theory as it applies to organizations. *Organization Development Journal, 21*(4), 50–64.

Lynch, K. (1960). *The image of the city*. Cambridge, MA: MIT Press.

Macneil, I.R. (1974). The many futures of contracts. *Southern California Law Review, 47*, 691–816.

Maheswaran, D., & Chaiken, S. (1991, July). Promoting systematic processing in low motivation settings: The effect of incongruent information on processing and judgment. *Journal of Personality and Social Psychology, 61*, 13–25.

Manufacturing & Logistics IT. (2009, January 15). GS1 UK backs industry initiative to standardise mobile scanning. http://www.logisticsit.com/absolutenm/templates/article-mobile.aspx?articleid=4365&zoneid=8, accessed on November 3, 2010.

Market Watch. (2011a, August 26). Poynt wins runner-up grand prize in Nokia's Calling All Innovators 2011 contest. Press Release. http://www.marketwatch.com/story/poynt-wins-runner-up-grand-prize-in-nokias-calling-all-innovators-2011-contest-2011–08–26, accessed on September 5, 2011.

Market Watch. (2011b, October 13). Smart Phone applications to surpass $15 billion. http://www.marketwatch.com/story/smart-phone-applications-to-surpass-15-billion-2011–10–13, accessed on October 19, 2011.

Mathieson, K. (1991). Predicting user intentions: Comparing the technology acceptance model with the theory of planned behavior. *Information Systems Research, 2*(3), 173–191.

Mathur, A., Chikkatur, A., & Sagar, A. (2007). Past as prologue: An innovation-diffusion approach to additionality. *Climate Policy, 7*(3), 230–239.

Mayer, R., Davis, J., & Schoorman, F.D. (1995, July). An integrative model of organizational trust. *Academy of Management Review, 20,* 709–734.

MediaPost. (2008, July 16). MMA issues mobile privacy guidelines. News. http://www.mediapost. com/publications/?fa=Articles.showArticle&art_aid=86663, accessed on February 2, 2010.

The Merriam-Webster Dictionary (2005). Springfield, MA: Merriam-Webster.

Miller, C.C. (2010). "E-Books Top Hardcovers at Amazon," *The New York Times,* New York edition, July 20, 2010, B1.

Miller, H.J. (2005). What about people in geographic information science? In P. Fisher & D. Unwin (Eds.), *Re-presenting geographical information systems* (pp. 215–242). New York: John Wiley & Sons.

Milne, G.R., & Gordon, M.E. (1994). Direct mail privacy-efficiency trade-offs within an implied social contract framework. *Journal of Public Policy & Marketing, 12*(2), 206–215.

MMA. (2008). Mobile marketing industry glossary. http://www.mmaglobal.com/glossary.pdf, accessed on June, 22, 2010.

MMA. (2009, November 17). MMA updates definition of mobile marketing. News. http://mma-global.com/news/mma-updates-definition-mobile-marketing, accessed on March 2, 2011.

MMA. (2010). Mobile commerce. MMA glossary. http://mmaglobal.com/wiki/mobile-commerce, accessed on September 2, 2011.

Mobile Commerce Daily (2011). McDonald's taps augmented reality, mobile check-ins for Smurfs promotion, August 3, http://www.mobilecommercedaily.com/2011/08/03/mcdonald%E2%80%99s-taps-augmented-reality-mobile-check-ins-for-smurfs-promotion. accessed on March 22, 2012.

Mobile Marketing. (2011, January 31). Red Bull proximity marketing campaign distributes mobile coupons via Bluetooth. http://www.mobilemarketer.com/cms/news/database-crm/8924.html, accessed on May 2, 2011.

Mobile Media Monitor. (2011, September 17). Japan mobile industry mulls 'Galapagos' effect. http://www.gilesrichter.com/2011/03/10/japanese-mobile-industry-ponders-galapagos-effect/, accessed on October 1, 2011.

Moehring, M., Lessig, C., & Bimber, O. (2004a). Optical tracking and video see-through AR on consumer cell phones. In *Proceedings of Workshop on Virtual and Augmented Reality of the GI-Fachgruppe AR/VR* (pp. 193–204).

Moehring, M., Lessig, C., & Bimber, O. (2004b). Video see-through AR on consumer cell phones. In *Proceedings of International Symposium on Augmented and Mixed Reality (ISMAR2004)* (pp. 252–253).

Montello, D.R., Waller, D., Hegarty, M., & Richardson, A.E. (2004). Spatial memory of real environments, virtual environments, and maps. In G.L. Allen (Ed.), *Human spatial memory: Remembering where* (pp. 251–285). Mahwah, NJ: Lawrence Erlbaum Associates.

Moorman, C., Deshpandé, R., & Zaltman G., (1993). Factors affecting trust in market research relationships. *Journal of Marketing, 57*(1), 81–101.

Muk, A. (2007) Consumers' intentions to opt in to SMS advertising: A cross-national study of young Americans and Koreans. *International Journal of Advertising, 26*(2), 177–198.

Nasco, S.A., & Bruner, G.C. (2008). Comparing consumer responses to advertising and non-advertising mobile communications. *Psychology & Marketing, 25*(8), 822–838.

New Media Age. (2008, May 8). Harrods uses QR codes for designer campaign. http://www.nma.co.uk/news/harrods-uses-qr-codes-for-designer-campaign/37907.article, accessed on July 2, 2011.

New Mexico State University. (2005, October 20). Retinal scans eyed for New Mexico show cattle. *ScienceDaily*, accessed on August 24, 2010.

NFC News (2010, September 2). Cimbal launches software-based mobile payment network. http://www.nfcnews.com/2010/09/02/cimbal-launches-software-based-mobile-payment-network, accessed on September 22, 2011.

Nielsenwire. (2010, August 2). Android soars, but iPhone still most desired as Smartphones grab 25% of U.S. mobile market. http://blog.nielsen.com/nielsenwire/online_mobile/android-soars-but-iphone-still-most-desired-as-smartphones-grab-25-of-u-s-mobile-market/, accessed on August 22, 2011.

Nielsenwire. (2011, May 31). Android leads in U.S. Smartphone market share and data usage. http://blog.nielsen.com/nielsenwire/consumer/android-leads-u-s-in-smartphone-market-share-and-data-usage/, accessed on June 2, 2011.

NTT DoCoMo. (2004). i-mode Ryokin Settei (i-mode charge list). Homepage. http://foma.nttdocomo.co.jp/charges/plan/i_mode/comini_05.html, accessed on June 28, 2010.

Nysveen, H., Pedersen, P.E., & Thorbjornsen, H. (2005). Intentions to use mobile services: Antecedents and cross-service comparisons. *Journal of the Academy of Marketing Science*, *33*(3), 330–346.

Oberauer, K., & Kliegl, R. (2004). Simultaneous cognitive operations in working memory after dual-task practice. *Journal of Experimental Psychology: Human Perception and Performance*, *30*(4), 689–707.

Okazaki, S. (2004). How do Japanese consumers perceive wireless ads? A multivariate analysis. *International Journal of Advertising*, *23*(4), 429–454.

Okazaki, S. (2006). What do we know about mobile Internet adopters? A cluster analysis. *Information & Management*, *43*(2), 127–141.

Okazaki, S., Katsukura, A., & Nishiyama, M. (2007). How mobile advertising works: The role of trust in improving attitudes and recall. *Journal of Advertising Research*, *47*(2), 165–178.

Okazaki, S., Li, H., & Hirose, M. (2009). Consumer privacy concerns and preference for degree of regulatory control: A study of mobile advertising in Japan. *Journal of Advertising*, *38*(4), 63–77.

Okazaki, S., Li, H., & Hirose, M. (2012). Benchmarking the use of QR code in mobile promotion: Three studies in Japan. *Journal of Advertising Research*, *52*(1), 1–16.

Okazaki, S., Skapa, R., & Grande, I. (2008). Capturing global youth: Mobile gaming in the US, Spain and the Czech Republic. *Journal of Computer-Mediated Communications*, *13*(4), 827–855.

Oliver, R.L. (1980). Cognitive model of the antecedents and consequences of satisfaction decisions. *Journal of Marketing Research*, *17*(4), 460–469.

Pagani, M. (2004). Determinants of adoption of third generation mobile multimedia services. *Journal of Interactive Marketing*, *18*(3), 46–59.

Pan, B., MacLaurin, T., & Crotts, J.C. (2007). Travel blogs and the implications for destination marketing. *Journal of Travel Research*, *46*, 135–145.

Parkes, D., & Thrift, N. (1980). *Times, spaces, and places: A chronogeographic perspective*. New York: John Wiley.

Parry, T. (2008). U ready 4 QR codes? *Multichannel Merchant*, *25*(10), 42.

Pascoe J. (1998). Adding generic contextual capabilities to wearable computers. In *Proceedings of the Second International Symposium on Wearable Computers (ISWC)* (pp. 92–99). Pittsburgh, PA: IEEE Computer Society.

Pashler, H. (2000). Task switching and multitask performance (tutorial). In S. Monsell & J. Driver (Eds.), *Control of cognitive processes: Attention and performance XVIII* (pp. 277–309). Cambridge, MA: The MIT Press.

Paul, I. (2009, September 2). Google's Gmail fail casts dark cloud on "cloud computing": Google dropped the "cloud computing" ball when Gmail failed Tuesday giving all Web services a black eye. PCWorld. http://www.pcworld.com/printable/article/id,171296/printable.html.

PCWorld (2009). Android vs. iPhone: Which Has the More Advanced Users? November 19, http://www.pcworld.com/article/182695/android_vs_iphone_which_has_the_more_advanced_users.html. accessed on September 21, 2011.

PCWorld. (2009, December 2). A hands-on tour: Google goggles visual search. Today@PCWorld. http://www.pcworld.com/article/183933/a_handson_tour_google_goggles_visual_search.html, accessed on March 22, 2011.

PCWorld. (2011a, August 2). Apple iCloud: What it is, and what it cost. *Today@PCWorld*. http://www.pcworld.com/article/237086/apple_icloud_what_it_is_and_what_it_costs.html, accessed on July 21, 2011.

PCWorld. (2011b, August 16). Apple's iAd platform: Success or failure? Apple launched the iAd platform to take on Google in mobile advertising, but after a couple months with iAds the reviews are mixed. http://www.pcworld.com/printable/article/id,203353/printable.html, accessed on October 4, 2011.

Pepper, B., Rueda-Sabater, E.J., Boeggeman, B.C., & Garrity, J. (2009). From mobility to ubiquity: Ensuring the power and promise of Internet connectivity . . . for anyone, anywhere, anytime. In S. Dutta & I. Mia (Eds.), *The global information technology report 2008–2009: Mobility in a networked world.* Geneva: World Economic Forum.

Peters, C., Amato, C.H., & Hollenbeck, C.R. (2007). An exploratory investigation of consumers' perceptions of wireless advertising. *Journal of Advertising, 36*(4), 129–145.

PhoCusWright. (2009). *The PhoCusWright consumer technology survey* (2nd ed.). Sherman, CT: PhoCusWright.

PluGGd.in. (2011, April 29). Mobile user privacy, LBS and the impact on App developers. http://www.pluggd.in/mobile-user-privacy-lbs-and-the-impact-on-app-developers-297/, accessed on July 24, 2011.

Pool, M.M., Koolstra, C.M., & van der Voort, T.H.A. (2003). Distraction effects of background soap operas on homework performance: An experimental study enriched with observational data. *Educational Psychology, 23*(4), 361–380.

Portio Research. (2011) *Mobile messaging futures 2011–2015.* Chippenham, UK: Portio Research.

Ptochos, D., Panopoulos, D., Metaxiotis, K., Askounis, D., & Psarras, J. (2004). Using Internet GIS technology for early warning, response, and controlling the quality of the public health sector. *International Journal on Electronic Healthcare, 1*(1), 78–102.

Radner, R., & Rothschild, M. (1975). On the allocation of effort. *Journal of Economic Theory, 10,* 358–376.

Raman, S. (2011, August 18). SMS: The dying cash cow for wireless carriers? FierceMobileContent. http://www.fiercemobilecontent.com/print/node/19711.

Reagan, G. (2011, March 2). See something, scan something: Bloomberg pushes QR codes. Capital. http://www.capitalnewyork.com/article/culture/2011/03/1506073/see-something-scan-something-bloomberg-pushes-qr-codes.

ReviseComputing.co.uk (2012). Commercial Data Processing, Bar code. *Glossaries*, http://www.revisecomputing.co.uk/sg_revision/glossaries/cdp_glossary.htm, accessed on January 12, 2012.

RFID Journal. (2004, September 7). Museum puts tags on stuffed birds. RFID News. http://www.rfidjournal.com/article/articleview/1110/1/1/, accessed on February 2, 2010.

Rice, R.E. (2009). Diffusion of innovations: Theoretical extensions. In R. Nabi & M.B. Oliver (Eds.), *Handbook of media effects* (pp. 489–503). Thousand Oaks, CA: Sage.

Rocchi, C., & Zancanaro, M. (2004). Rhetorical patterns for adaptive video documentaries. In W. Nejdl & P. De Bra (Eds.), *Adaptive hypermedia and adaptive web-based systems* (pp. 324–327). Berlin: Springer-Verlag.

Rodriguez-Perlado, V.R., & Barwise, P. (2004). Mobile advertising: A research agenda. In M.R. Stafford & R.J. Faber (Eds.), *Advertising, promotion, and new media* (pp. 261–277). Armonk, NY: M.E. Sharpe.

Rogers, E.M. (1976). New product adoption and diffusion. *Journal of Consumer Research, 2*(4), 290–301.

Rogers, E.M. (1995). *Diffusion of innovations* (4th ed.). New York: The Free Press.

Rotter, Julian B. (1971). Generalized expectancies for interpersonal trust. *American Psychologist, 26*, 443–452.

Rouillard, J. (2008). Contextual QR codes. *Proceedings of the Third International Multi-Conference on Computing in the Global Information Technology. ICCGI 2008*. CD-ROM.

Rubin, A.M. (1983). Television uses and gratifications: The interactions of viewing patterns and motivations. *Journal of Broadcasting, 27*(1), 37–51.

Rubinstein, J.S., Meyer, D.E., & Evans, J.E. (2001). Executive control of cognitive processes in task switching. *Journal of Experimental Psychology: Human Perception and Performance, 27*(4), 763–797.

Sadeh, N. (2002). *M-commerce: Technologies, services, and business models*. New York: John Wiley & Sons.

Schwanen, T., & Kwan, M.P. (2008). The Internet, mobile phone and space-time constraints. *Geoforum, 39*(3), 1362–1377.

Search Engine Watch. (2011, January 14). Will search drive mobile ad revenues? http://searchenginewatch.com/article/2063940/Will-Search-Drive-Mobile-Ad-Revenues, accessed on May 2, 2011.

SET. (2009, April 14). Louis Vuitton choose SET Japan for latest QR marketing push. http://www.set-japan.com/qrcode/louis-vuitton-qr-code/?lang=en, accessed on July 31, 2011.

Shahriyar, R., Md. Faizul, B., Gourab, K., Sheikh, I.A., & Md. Mostofa, A. (2009). Intelligent Mobile Health Monitoring System (IMHMS). *International Journal of Control and Automation, 2*(3), 13–28.

Sharma, A., Wingfield, N., & Yuan, L. (2007, February 17). How Steve Jobs played hardball in iPhone birth. *The Wall Street Journal*, p. A1.

Sharma, C., & Nakamura, Y. (2003). *Wireless data services: Business models and global markets*. Cambridge: Cambridge University Press.

Sharsky, M. (2009). Bluetooth technology at the airport: What if your mobile phone got you through security lines faster? Bluetooth. http://www.bluetooth.com/English/Experience/Pages/Help_Speed_Airport_Security_Lines.aspx, accessed on March 21, 2011.

Shaw, S-L., & Yu, H. (2009). A GIS-based time-geographic approach of studying individual activities and interactions in a hybrid physical-virtual space. *Journal of Transport Geography, 17,* 141–149.

Sheehan, K.B., & Hoy, M.G. (1999). Flaming, complaining, abstaining: How online users respond to privacy concerns. *Journal of Advertising, 28*(3), 37–51.

Sheeran, P., & Taylor, S. (1999). Predicting intentions to use condoms: A meta-analysis and comparison of the theories of reasoned action and planned behavior. *Journal of Applied Social Psychology, 29,* 1624–1675.

Sheppard, B.H., Hartwick, J., & Warshaw, P.R. (1988). The theory of reasoned action: A meta-analysis of past research with recommendations for modifications and future research. *Journal of Consumer Research, 15*(3), 325–343.

Sparks, B.A., & Browning, V. (2011). The impact of online reviews on hotel booking intentions and perception of trust. *Tourism Management, 32*(6), 1310–1323.

Stafford, T.F., Stafford, M.R., & Schkade, L.L. (2004). Determining uses and gratifications for the Internet. *Decision Sciences, 35*(2), 259–288.

Stock, O., Zancanaro, M., Busetta, P., Callaway, C., Krüger, A., Kruppa, M., Kuflik, T., Not, E., & Rocchi, C. (2007). Adaptive, intelligent presentation of information for the museum visitor in PEACH. *User Modeling and User-Adapted Interaction, 17*(3), 257–304.

Sutter, J.D. (2010, October 18). Smartphones: Our national obsession. CNN Tech. http://articles.cnn.com/2010–10–18/tech/smartphone.everywhere_1_smartphone-text-message-ipod/3?_s=PM:TECH.

Sutton, S. (1998). Predicting and explaining intentions and behavior: How well are we doing? *Journal of Applied Social Psychology, 28,* 1317–1338.

Szajna, B. (1996). Empirical evaluation of the revised technology acceptance model. *Management Science, 42*(1), 85–92.

Taft, D.K. (2011, June 20). Moving to the cloud: A "rational" choice for McDonald's. eWeek.com. http://www.eweek.com/c/a/Cloud-Computing/Moving-to-the-Cloud-a-Rational-Choice-for-McDonalds-864780/.

Taylor, S., & Todd, P.A. (1995). Understanding information technology usage: A test of competing models. *Information Systems Research, 6*(2), 144–176.

Thompson, R.L., Higgins, C.A., & Howell, J.M. (1991). Personal computing: Towards a conceptual model of utilisation. *MIS Quarterly, 14,* 125–143.

Tomlinson, J. (2004). Culture, modernity and immediacy. In U. Beck, N. Sznaider, & R. Winter (Eds.), *Global America?: The cultural consequences of globalization* (pp. 49–64). Liverpool: Liverpool University Press.

TripAdvisor. (2011). TripAdvisor hotels flights restaurants. http://itunes.apple.com/us/app/tripadvisor/id284876795?mt=8, accessed on September 1, 2011.

Tsang, M., Ho, S., & Liang, T. (2004). Consumer attitudes toward mobile advertising: An empirical study. *International Journal of Electronic Commerce, 8*(3), 65–78.

U.K. Parliamentary Office of Science and Technology (2004, July). Radio frequency identification (RFID). *Postnote, 225,* 1–4.

Ullah, S., Higgin, H., Arif Siddiqui, H., & Sup Kwak, K. (2008). A study of implanted and wearable body sensor networks. In N.T. Nguyen (Ed.), *KES-AMSTA 2008, LNAI 4953* (pp. 464–473). Berlin: Springer-Verlag.

Urquhart, K., Cartweight, W., Miller, S., Mitchell, K., & Benda, P. (2004). Exploring the usefulness of cartographic representations for location-based services in an Austrian context. *Journal of Spatial Science, 49*(1), 71–87.

Vallacher, R.R., & Wegner, D.M. (1987). What do people think they're doing? Action identification and human behavior. *Psychological Review, 94*, 3–15.

Van Halteren, A., Bults, R., Wac, K., Konstantas, D., Widya, I., Dokovsky, N., Koprinkov, G., Jones, V., & Herzog, R. (2004). Mobile patient monitoring: The MobiHealth system. *Information Technology in Healthcare, 2*(5), 365–373.

Van Halteren, A., Konstantas, D., Bults, R., Wac, K., Dokovsky, N., Koprinkov, G., Jones, V., & Widya, I. (2004). Mobihealth: Ambulant patient monitoring over next generation public wireless networks. *Studies in Health Technology and Informatics, 106*, 107–122.

Vance, J. (2009, May 13). Will desktop virtualization and the rise of netbooks kill the PC? Internet.com. http://itmanagement.earthweb.com/netsys/article.php/3820161, accessed on July 21, 2011.

Venkatesh, V. (2000). Determinants of perceived ease of use: Integrating control, intrinsic motivation, and emotion into the technology acceptance model. *Information Systems Research, 11*(4), 342–365.

Venkatesh, V. (2003). Mobile commerce opportunities and challenges: Understanding usability in mobile commerce. *Communications of the ACM, 46*(12).

Venkatesh, V., & Bala, H. (2008). Technology acceptance model 3 and a research agenda on interventions. *Decision Science, 39*(2), 273–315.

Venkatesh, V., & Davis, F.D. (1996). A model of the antecedents of perceived ease of use: Development and test. *Decision Science, 27*(3), 451–481.

Venkatesh, V., & Davis, F.D. (2000). A theoretical extension of the technology acceptance model: Four longitudinal field studies. *Management Science, 46*(2), 186–204.

Venkatesh, V., Morris, M.G., Davis, G.B., & Davis, F.D. (2003). User acceptance of information technology: Toward a unified view. *MIS Quarterly, 27*(3), 425–478.

Venkatesh, V., & Ramesh, V. (2006). Web and wireless site usability: Understanding differences and modeling use. *MIS Quarterly, 30*(1), 181–206.

Vroom, V. (1982). *Work and motivation.* New York: John Wiley & Sons.

Wac, K., Bargh, M., van Beijnum, B.J., Bults, R., Pawar, P., & Peddemors, A. (2009). Power- and delay-awareness of health telemonitoring services: The MobiHealth system case study. *IEEE JSAC, Special Issue on Wireless and Pervasive Communications in Healthcare, 27*(4), 1–12.

Wang, Y., Aroyo, L., Stash, N., Sambeek, R., Schuurmans Y., Schreiber, G., & Gorgels, P. (2009). Cultivating Personalized Museum Tours Online and On-Site, *Journal of Interdisciplinary Science Reviews, 34*(2), 141–156.

Watson, R.T., Pitt, L.F., Berthon, P., & Zinkhan, G.M. (2002). U-commerce: Expanding the universe of marketing. *Journal of the Academy of Marketing Science, 30*(4), 333–347.

Weiser, M. (1993). Some computer science issues in ubiquitous computing. *Communication of the ACM, 361*(7), 75–84.

Westin, A.F. (1967). *Privacy and freedom,* New York: Atheneum.

Whang, L.S.M., & Chang, G. (2004). Lifestyles of virtual world residents: Living in the on-line game "Lineage." *CyberPsychology & Behavior, 7*(5), 592–600.

Wilson, T.V. (2007, June 20). How the iPhone works. Tech. HowStuffWorks. http://electronics.howstuffworks.com/iphone.htm, accessed on July 23, 2011.

Wireless World Research Forum (WWRF). (2001). Book of visions 2001: Visions of the wireless world—version 1.0. http://duda.imag.fr/edu/WWRF-book-of-vision.pdf, accessed on July 23, 2010.

Wixom, B. H., & Todd, P. A. (2005). A theoretical integration of user satisfaction and technology acceptance. *Information Systems Research*, 16(1), 85–102.

W3C. (2011). Standards. http://www.w3.0rg/, accessed on July 23, 2011.

Wu, J.H., & Wang, S.C. (2005). What drives mobile commerce? An empirical evaluation of the revised technology acceptance model. *Information & Management*, 42(5), 719–729.

WWRF (2001). *The Book of Visions 2001: Visions of the Wireless World, Version 1.0*, Wireless World Research Forum, December 2001; http://www.wireless-world-research.org/

Xia, J., Packer, D., & Dong, C. (2009). Individual differences and tourist wayfinding behaviours. *18th World IMACS/MODSIM Congress*. Cairns, Australia. July 13–17. http://mssanz.org.au/modsim09, accessed on October 2, 2011.

Xiang, Z., & Gretzel, U. (2010). Role of social media in online travel information search. *Tourism Management*, 31(2), 179–188.

The Yomiuri Shimbun (2008). *Survey on city dwellers in 2008*. Tokyo: Yomiuri Shimbun (in Japanese).

Yu, H. (2006). Spatio-temporal GIS design for exploring interactions of human activities. *Cartography and Geographic Information Science*, 33(1), 3–19.

Zancanaro, M., Kuflik, T., Boger, Z., Goren-Bar, D., & Goldwasser, D. (2007). Analyzing museum visitors' behavior patterns. In C. Conati, K. McCoy, & G. Paliouras (Eds.), *User modeling* (pp. 238–246). Berlin: Springer-Verlag.

ZDNet. (2008, January 11). 56% of Americans use SMS, 33% see ads on cell phones. IT Facts. http://www.zdnet.com/blog/itfacts/56-of-americans-use-sms-33-see-ads-on-cell-phones/13615?tag=btxcsim, accessed on June 3, 2010.

ZDNet. (2011, August 9). Would you trust Google with your wallet? http://www.zdnet.com/blog/google/would-you-trust-google-with-your-wallet/3219, accessed on September 22, 2011.

Zhang, J., & Mao, E. (2008). Understanding the acceptance of mobile SMS advertising among young Chinese consumers. *Psychology & Marketing*, 25(8), 787–805.

Index